CHINA'S
RELIGIOUS
HERITAGE

CHINA'S
RELIGIOUS
HERITAGE

Y. C. YANG

President, Soochow University, China, and
Tallman Professor of Chinese Civilization
Bowdoin College, Maine

ABINGDON-COKESBURY PRESS
New York • Nashville

CHINA'S RELIGIOUS HERITAGE
COPYRIGHT, MCMXLIII
BY WHITMORE & STONE

SET UP, PRINTED, AND BOUND BY THE PARTHENON PRESS AT NASHVILLE, TENNESSEE, UNITED STATES OF AMERICA

DEDICATED TO

Bishop Arthur J. Moore

*President of Board of Missions and Church
Extension of The Methodist Church
Bishop of China Conference, 1934-1940*

An Inspiring Leader
World-Wide in Vision, Untiring in Effort
Devoted in Service, and
Brotherly in Love

Dr. W. B. Nance

*Now for forty-two years in service at
Soochow University
President Emeritus, Adviser, Professor of Philosophy*

A Respected Teacher, an Intimate Friend
And an Eminent Colleague Among My Esteemed Associates
in the University

Dr. Fred P. Manget, M.D.

*For over thirty years the superintendent of
Huchow General Hospital*

Beloved Physician "of China"
A Distinguished Member Among the
Great Band of Noble Missionaries
Who Love the Chinese More Than
They Care for Themselves

PREFACE

If the moving finger of time has done any sky-writing for this age and generation it is in the public announcement that mankind has moved on from the stage of regional existence to a condition of basic world unity. However we may be devoted to our "hall of independence," we must bear in mind that it is now located on the grand concourse of interdependence.

The family of nations, in spite of its all too many quarrels and apparent divisions which disturb its harmony and tranquillity, is no longer a phrase but a *fait accompli*. Permanent improvement, however, will not likely be achieved until nations and peoples can be taught to meet each other on the higher plane of cultural understanding and spiritual fellowship. This is pre-eminently the task of education and religion.

Religion in modern times, therefore, must have a broader conception of its mission and function. Besides dealing with the individuals it must take a larger and more active interest in the cultures and civilizations of the world. Christianity, if it is indeed to be the salt of the earth, must know, with reference to the other living religions in the world, wherefore it is the indispensable salt and wherein the other great systems of religion need to be salted.

Paradoxical as it may seem, the first step in leading the other religions to an understanding and appreciation of Christianity is for Christians themselves to exert their effort toward a fuller understanding and better appreciation of the merits and true worth of the other religions. Speaking concretely and with particular reference to China, we may conclude that the best and most effective way to help the Chinese to know Christ and appreciate Christianity is for the Christians to have a true understanding and proper appreciation of the cultural and religious heritage of China. It is only thus that Christianity can go on "to fulfill" rather than "to destroy," for only with that preparation can it know when and how to say, "Yea, yea," and "Nay, nay."

This task is supremely important because, from the point of view of Christian missions, China today is a strategic point at a psychological moment. The unchanging China is becoming an all-changing China. China is rediscovering not only her West but also her past, and is once more readjusting her bearings to fit into a newer and larger environ-

8

ment. Indeed, she is seeking a new life to live in a new world.

Fundamentally speaking, of all the great battles which have taken place and may take place in her heroic resistance against military aggression, none can compare in real significance and far-reaching consequence with the "battle of the future" which is going on in the realm of the thought and faith of her people. Nothing is stopping the birth of a new nation. The "incident" which was designed to be a knockout blow will pass off as an incident. But this New China will be molded and shaped by the vision which she will see, the faith which she will embrace, and the God whom she will worship. Therefore, an understanding of what is going on in the minds of the people is the key to understanding the great national movements which are and will be going on in the country. Christianity must hold this key in order to know the best approach in bringing Christ to China and China to Christ.

This little book represents an honest and sincere effort to evaluate and interpret the cultural and religious heritage of the Chinese alongside of Christianity. It gives a very brief survey of the teachings and essential features of Confucianism, Buddhism, and Taoism, which have been traditionally spoken of as "the three religions of China," and

9

compares them with each other and with Christianity.

The author did not start out with the preconceived objective either to exalt the virtues of Chinese culture or to demonstrate the supremacy of Christianity. But, as a result of this further study and investigation, he has come out not only with an enhanced appreciation of the religious heritage of the Chinese but also with a deepened conviction that when Jesus Christ said to the Samaritan woman, "Whosoever drinketh of this water shall thirst again: but whosoever drinketh of the water that I shall give him shall never thirst," he was uttering a Gospel truth applicable to all ages and all peoples.

As far as the author is aware, no book in English on the religions of China has yet been written by a Chinese. In fact, he does not even know of a book in Chinese which covers the same scope and has the same perspective. The author is not a theologian, nor a philosopher, but just another "plain man" who, as Professor Henry P. Van Dusen says, "seeks for God." He does not pretend to be an authority on the subject, but he hopes that his book may have some small contribution to make and may be interesting because he is an ordinary layman and because, being a Chinese, he had easier access to original Chinese sources of information and was able to catch the spirit and the atmosphere and sense the situation in a way not possible to Western writers.

This volume is based upon a series of lectures on the Quillian Foundation which the author had the honor of delivering at Emory University, in January, 1942. He therefore wishes to express his thanks to President Cox and Dean Trimble of Emory University for having honored him with the invitation, to Professor Arva C. Floyd, chairman of the Ministers' Week Committee, and also to the audience for their most gracious and encouraging reception. In the preparation of this book the author received much valuable help from the published works of many Western writers who have dealt with one or more phases of this general subject; but more particularly he wishes to acknowledge his indebtedness to Professor Robert E. Hume of Union Theological Seminary, New York, an inspiring teacher and eminent authority on comparative religion, for valuable advice and suggestions; to Dr. William F. Quillian and Dr. Elmer T. Clark, always his good and helpful friends; and to Dr. M. O. Williams, Jr., and Mr. J. W. Dyson, his intimate and esteemed colleagues in Soochow University.

Y. C. YANG

Brunswick, Me.

CONTENTS

1

THE RELIGIOUS SIGNIFICANCE
OF CHINESE CULTURE

I. THE FUNDAMENTAL PROBLEM OF CHRISTIAN MISSIONS

As the Bible is the common textbook and the standard reference for all Christians, it seems appropriate, in introducing a discussion of China's religious heritage and the proper Christian attitude toward it, to refer briefly to two very familiar passages in the Holy Scriptures in which we see the whole problem of missions—its starting point and its ultimate objective.

The first of these has to do with the story, in the Gospel according to St. John, of Jesus and the Samaritan woman at the well of Sychar.[1] When the woman heard Jesus speaking of the living water he could give, she asked our Lord this very poignant and challenging question :"Art thou greater than our father Jacob?"

The second reference is to a few verses in the

[1] John 4:10-15.

15

Gospel according to St. Matthew.[2] Here Simon Peter, in answering the question which Jesus put to his disciples, "But whom say ye that I am?" said, "Thou art the Christ, the Son of the living God."

In these two passages we see the whole story of missions: the first problem it has to face, the proper method of approach, the secret of effective preaching, and the mark of genuine conversion. "Art thou greater than our father Jacob?" is the great query of the non-Christian world when confronted with Jesus Christ as the Saviour for all mankind, and not simply a prophet for some particular nation or race only. "Thou art the Christ, the Son of the living God," is the great revelation, the great confession—that knowledge and conviction which it is the great commission of the Christian church to bring to man everywhere.

The first passage contains the question of the non-Christian inquirer; the second passage presents the answer of Christian faith.

Every people have their "father Jacob," who has left them "a well" from which he drank, and his children and their cattle after him. In him they have reposed reverence and confidence; from him they have been drawing their inspiration; to him they have been looking for guidance; and he, in their esteem and in their judgment, has been super-

[2] Matt. 16:13-16.

16

latively important, an overtowering figure and a matchless leader. When we, as Christians, present to such other people our Lord Jesus Christ and his Gospel, calling upon them to repent and give up their religion, to turn away from their gods and their prophets, and accept our God and his Christ, it is fair and natural that they should want to know and be convinced that our Christ is really greater than their "father Jacob."

One of the reasons why Jesus Christ was able to impress upon the Samaritan woman the validity and authority of his words was the fact that she sensed that Jesus knew all about their father Jacob and his well; and yet, with full knowledge and appreciation of who Jacob was—indeed, because of that very knowledge—he could say with confidence and certainty that he had something very much better to give. "Whosoever drinketh of this water shall thirst again: but whosoever drinketh of the water that I shall give him shall never thirst." "Ye worship ye know not what: we know what we worship." Positive and unequivocal! Full of grace and full of truth! The woman was moved with the conviction that Jesus was verily a prophet; she believed that he was the Christ, because she perceived that he could tell men all things.

So it is with us in our ministry to all the "Samaritans" of the world—the Confucianists, the Buddhists, and the Taoists and what not. We must also be able to answer to their satisfaction that our Christ is greater than their Jacob. But surely we cannot give an intelligent answer or even an honest opinion, much less any convincing assurance, if we do not know who their Jacob is, nor anything about his well. A very familiar Chinese proverb has it that to be always assured of success one must know the one he deals with as well as himself.

This knowledge of their father Jacob and his well is particularly important when we preach to the non-Christians—this is especially true when we deal with them as groups and not just as individuals. In most cases we are not dealing with persons who have absolutely nothing to start with, but are advising them to give up something which they usually hold very valuable, in favor of something else which we claim is to be infinitely better. But not even a child would believe us if he knew that we had no idea of what he had to start with.

This point is particularly pertinent when we deal with the Christian movement in China. When Christianity was introduced into China, it did not go into a field which was entirely vacant and uncultivated. In the spiritual and cultural realm, as in the material and physical world, China has its Yangtse Delta which is even richer than the famous

18

delta of the Nile. Christianity found in China a nation already in possession of a culture and a civilization which had been brought up to a high state of development. It had inherited a fairly sound moral system, well seasoned with good practical common sense. The Chinese philosophy of life had laid its main emphasis on the ideal rather than the material, on the spiritual rather than the physical. The religions and religious institutions of the Chinese had already become deeply rooted in the life and customs of the people.

Their culture and civilization was in many respects different from the Western Christian culture and civilization, but nevertheless it was a genuine culture and an advanced civilization. And, if we judge the tree by its fruits, it was not such a bad one either; for the life values and spiritual assets held in esteem by the Chinese, the ideal of manhood they were taught to honor, and the type of man actually produced, were not altogether low and mean, but, on the whole, quite presentable and honorable. The Chinese social structure and organization had produced good order and stability and a set of *mores* which could meet fairly high ethical standards. The spiritual heritage of the Chinese people was so deeply rooted that one could not blow it away with a puff of the breath; it was so rich in content that one could not brush it aside

19

with a casual sweep of the hand. It could not, and should not, be totally discarded without a careful examination, a fair evaluation, and a discriminating selection.

Therefore, he who wants to guide the Chinese must start by understanding them; he who wants to teach the Chinese must first learn what they have already been taught. The beginning of an understanding of the problem of evangelization and the discovery of the best method of giving Christianity to China lies in a careful survey of her spiritual heritage and religious background and a discerning appraisal of its true worth and value.

In the early days of the modern Christian movement in China, there was a strong current of opinion which held that there was nothing in the religions of China but blind ignorance and superstitious idolatry. Those holding such views were ready to declare the whole thing worthless and useless and were ready to knock it down with one general condemnation. All the three religions of China—Confucianism, Buddhism, Taoism—were looked upon and condemned as three fortresses or citadels of Satan which must be completely demolished. With the Canaanites there should be no compromise: their altars must be destroyed, their images broken and their groves cut, whether they were of the Amorites, the Hittites, or the Jebusites. Christianity was out for a conquest. It was a conquest of love, to be sure, but nevertheless it was to be a conquest.

As we look over the pages of history in the light of the present day, with its longer experience and better understanding, we now can see that there was much in the Christian movement of the nineteenth century which indicates a battle of blind prejudice on both sides. Because of bad technique and poor tactics—which, in the natural course of things, could not be entirely avoided—much of love's labor was thereby lost. The good will and enthusiasm of the early Christian effort in China was met, for the most part, with scornful indifference by the learned and the intelligent.

Gradually, through increasing contacts, there came a better knowledge of China's religions as foreign observers began to penetrate the crust of outward formality and ceremonial rite to a deeper significance. This better knowledge led to a truer understanding of their underlying philosophy and basic beliefs, so that wholesale condemnation gradually gave way to growing appreciation. Christians began to see that in the religions and philosophy of the Chinese there are many beautiful gems of noble truth which are strikingly similar to the teachings of Jesus Christ. At the same time, non-Christians began to see the beauty of the Christian

21

ideals and admire the spirit of love and service clearly reflected in the lives of the noble band of devoted missionaries. A change of attitude took place, and better relations prevailed. To this better understanding and deeper knowledge of China the Sinologues, who were mostly pioneer missionaries, made very valuable contributions through their scholarly research and sympathetic approach. Knowledge led to understanding; understanding produced appreciation; appreciation generated enthusiasm.

In some cases today Christians of the West have seen so much in the beautiful ideals and rich philosophy found in the Oriental religions, and have become so impressed with the practical wisdom of Confucius, the remarkable psychological insight of Buddhism, and the sublime, though subtle, philosophy of Taoism, that they have tended to go to the other extreme of being even a little too liberal and too compromising.

For instance, there are some who take the position that the main purpose of Christian missions in entering the non-Christian field is to co-operate in a joint research for universal truth. There are some others who maintain that all religions should perhaps co-exist, and should mutually learn from each other. To them it seems that both Christianity and some of the more highly developed non-

Christian religions possess much truth, but that neither the one nor the other is wholly beyond illusion.

To keep ourselves from being thrown off our balance by either the careless, wholesale condemnation of the one, or the overenthusiastic appreciation of the other, we should exercise a discerning understanding of the nature and content of the ethnic religions, and a critical analysis of the points of strength and weakness in each. We must be fair to others, but also be sure of ourselves. Both positions call for a knowledge of the basic facts of the non-Christian religions, in order that we may make intelligent comparisons. Such knowledge will not only enable us to meet others with a fair appreciation of their point of view and thus win both their friendship and their confidence, but will also strengthen our faith in our own religion, so that with a knowledge of the imperfections, incompleteness, and impotency of all other religions, we are all the more sure of the unsearchable riches of Christ "that filleth all in all," and the fullness of God who "is able to do exceeding abundantly above all that we ask or think." It is only when we are thus equipped in knowledge and strengthened in faith that we can "run, not as uncertainly; so fight . . . , not as one that beateth the air." It is only thus that we can fully comprehend the centrality and

23

the finality of our Christ and his Gospel, and lead others to see that his name is verily above all other names, and that his gift of life is experientially better than anything else which life can offer.

The question of how to deal with the ethnic religions is not a new problem, nor one which is limited to China alone. There have always been two rather conflicting views on the subject. There have been those who insisted rigorously that "there is none other name under heaven given among men, whereby we must be saved" [3] and that "no man hath seen God at any time; the only begotten Son, which is in the bosom of the Father, he hath declared him." [4] Those who stressed such passages usually maintained not only that Christ was the only Way of Salvation, but that he was the only Revelation of God. "No man cometh unto the Father, but by me." [5] He was the Light which shineth in the darkness. Outside of him was total darkness. He was not only the Great Light and Perfect Light, but the Only Light. Aside from him there were not even broken lights; there was no light whatsoever.

Religions could be separated, as it were, by a true and false classification test. Christianity was the

[3] Acts 4:12.
[4] John 1:18.
[5] John 14:6.

24

only true religion; all others were but false religions. There was no point of contact between Christianity and the other religions of the world. Outside of the revelation of God by Christ in the Bible— the "Biblical realism" of Kraemer—there was no other revelation of God anywhere else or at any other time. The one business and concern of Christian missions and evangelism, therefore, should be to understand Christian revelation and to proclaim it to the world. There is no true value in any of the non-Christian religions.

But, against this, there are persons who follow another line of thought, built on another series of the passages from the Holy Scriptures. They recalled that Paul, the pre-eminent apostle to the Gentiles, and who therefore could speak on the subject with particular authority, had told the Lycaonians that God "in times past suffered all nations to walk in their own ways. Nevertheless he left not himself without witness." [6] In the Epistle to the Hebrews we are told that He who spoke to us by his Son in the last days had "at sundry times and in divers manners spake in time past unto the fathers by the prophets." [7] Jesus also said that he did not "come to destroy the law, or the prophets:

[6] Acts 14:16.
[7] Heb. 1:1.

25

. . . . but to fulfill," [8] and that after him there would come the Comforter, which is the Holy Spirit, whom the Father would send in his name, who would teach men all things.[9]

These passages seem to indicate that in addition to the great truths which Christ himself revealed to his disciples, there could be and were other revelations of truth, preliminary and supplementary to, in preparation for and in explanation of the central truths which our Lord Jesus Christ came to reveal and give to the world. That the Gentiles could have the right kind of faith seemed to be evident from the reference which Jesus Christ made to the centurion, concerning whom he said, "I have not found so great faith, no, not in Israel." [10]

This discussion really resolves itself into two fundamental questions. First, did God, at any time, in any manner or degree, reveal himself to anybody besides Jesus and the Jewish prophets? No true Christian should doubt that God did, in a very unique and special way, reveal himself in Jesus Christ, who is the Light of the world, and the Way and the Truth for mankind. But if God is the God of all times and of all peoples, we can hardly imagine that he has confined all revelation to that short

[8] Matt. 5:17.
[9] John 14:26.
[10] Matt. 8:10.

26

period of time between Bethlehem and Calvary, and only to that small group of people in Palestine, leaving all other ages and all other peoples utterly devoid of his light. God's love and care for mankind transcends time and space, and is immanent in all peoples and all ages. He has not left himself without witness anywhere. In the saints and prophets of other lands and other religions he has also revealed himself to man.

Second, what is the nature of revelation? Is it a single act, or a continuous process? In other words, is God's revelation a gradual unfolding of his purpose, like the breaking of the dawn which slowly transforms the darkness of night into the brightness of the day, or is it like a sudden flash of lightning or a meteor shooting across the skies? Does God wait for a grand occasion and then speak, or does he continually teach mankind, by steps and by stages—speaking to us as a child when we are in the stage of childhood, and in more mature terms as we grow in general intelligence and in our knowledge of God?

For a person to insist that there is no value or truth in the non-Christian religions, and that therefore they can be ignored entirely, it would be necessary for him, besides answering the two above questions in a way to suit his theory, to maintain that not only is Christianity the sole custodian or

27

depository of all the truths but that it has perfect apprehension of the whole truth. But whole truths are for the whole of mankind. If so, would they not be better and more fully understood if stated or interpreted in terms of the universal experience of all mankind, instead of merely the experience of one people and one civilization?

The teachings of Christianity might be better understood by those to whom we are bringing the Gospel if the Bible should be translated into three versions—a word version, a thought version, and a life version. To turn the Bible from one language into another, word for word and phrase for phrase, is simply the beginning of making its teachings understood; for its deeper meaning and greater significance cannot be successfully conveyed until its teachings are successfully expressed in idea forms and thought units with which the people are familiar. The thought version of Christian teaching must be expressed in terms of the philosophy and religious experience of the people, comparing and contrasting the two, showing how and wherein they either agree or differ. Only in this way can the word be made both clear and vivid. The life version, of course, is the Acts of the Apostles—not only in the apostolic age, but in all succeeding ages—through which the word becomes flesh.

There need be no apprehension that in following

this procedure we are in danger of compromising our position, or allowing pagan conceptions to filter in to adulterate the purity of Christian ideas. For, to know what others believe, is not to believe what others claim to know. To recognize that there are certain values in the other religions does not necessarily mean attributing the same value to such religions. Our primary objective is not to search for equivalents, but for points of contact and for bases on which we can build the best explanation; thus may we more easily lead others on from their partial knowledge to a more adequate knowledge, and from an inadequate faith to a more adequate faith.

In comparison with Christianity, all other religions fall short and are incomplete. They all have to be adjusted and corrected, and their truth can be completed and fulfilled only in Christianity; but it is not necessarily true to say that they are wrong *in toto* and *ab initio*. A person who has lost the way is not necessarily in the wrong direction altogether. A student working on a problem in mathematics may commit certain errors which, if not corrected, will give him the wrong answer; but it is probably not necessary to condemn all that he has done. Much perhaps can be preserved. The best teaching method is to try discerningly to follow out his own line of thought, correcting him

29

where he needs to be corrected, and guiding him where he needs to be guided, thus putting him on the right track and enabling him to get the right answer. Can we not consider Christianity as the higher education of life, for which Confucianism and Buddhism have given men more or less of a secondary-school preparation?

Among the ethnic religions of the world, the group active in China is, from certain points of view, the most important as well as the most interesting. Familiarity with this group is not only important for Christian work in China, but there are reasons to think that it also has considerable bearing on the future of Christianity in the larger task of its world mission. A few of these reasons may be briefly mentioned.

1. China is a goodly part of the world; and the Chinese constitute about one fourth of the human race. Religions which influence this vast body of people have thus an important place in the total human scene.

2. China is not only imposing because of her size and numbers; she is perhaps the best exponent of Oriental civilization, one of the main currents in the cultural stream of the world. Her spiritual outlook and religious faith are important factors in the life of mankind.

3. The religious situation of China is intensely

interesting in that she has developed two religions of her own, Confucianism and Taoism, and has absorbed a third, Buddhism. Buddhism is one of the three religions in the world which aim to be universal, and it has actually become international. Together, these three religions have a following of only about a million less than the total number of Christians in the whole world.

4. China is the common meeting ground of four of the five great religions which have over one hundred million adherents each. Besides the three great religions named above, there are two others, namely, Mohammedanism and Christianity, which are in active force in China—the former in force of numbers, and the latter in force of influence. Hinduism may be regarded as indirectly present in China through the medium of Buddhism.

5. These five religions claim the allegiance of over three fourths of mankind. If Christianity, therefore, can find an effective way of dealing with the total religious situation of China, it will probably discover a satisfactory working formula for dealing with all the religions of the world.

This situation is particularly significant at the present time, when human history is moving into a distinctly new era; when mankind is no longer living in regional units—be it the nation, the continent, or the hemisphere—but in world unity. Mankind has

31

met at the crossroads of the world; and all parties will go down the road of history together. The Far East is no longer far, nor is it separated from the West. In order that the nations of the world may be a family, where beautiful family unity prevails, undisturbed by constant family quarrels, there must be a meeting of minds in fundamental ideals and basic conceptions of life. There is no more vital spot or happier ground for this all-important meeting than to meet in Christ before God. In order to bring this about, Christianity must hereafter deal not only with persons but with religions. This is not a type of futuristic idealism, but realism of the most fundamental and urgent sort. It is not distant speculation, but an essential part of the most immediate concern in the solution of the present world situation.

In this new world situation and all that it involves in the building of a new world culture and the construction of a new world order, the Far East will play a more important role and take a more active part than ever before. The most outstanding characteristic of the history of the nineteenth century was the action of the West upon the East. One of the most interesting things for the twentieth century to witness may well be the reaction of the East upon the West, and the interplay of the cultural forces and spiritual influences of both sides. In this, religion has an important part to play; for religion, by its very nature, deals with fundamentals—the universal, the comprehensive, and the eternal. The basis of world order is culture; and the essence of culture is religion. It is only when men meet in religion and in God that they can meet in fellowship and in brotherhood. This is the great central reality in comparison with which all other things are but superficial realities. For the people of the world to understand each other and to be united religiously is the problem of all problems.

How do China and the Far East fit into this picture? What is at stake and how will the world as a whole be affected by it? Prof. Oscar M. Buck, in his book *Christianity Tested*, written after two special trips to the Far East, says in the Preface: "The future of the Christian religion is being determined in Asia. The continent of Asia, with fifty-five per cent of the total population of the world, still lies unconvinced across the path of Christianity's claim to be the universal faith to which all races and peoples must come in time." He said that Christianity had its first great test in Europe during the first three centuries of the Christian era, and that it is now entering upon its second historical test in Asia. So great is the issue involved that "it is in Asia—not in America, or

33

Europe, or Africa—that the future of the Christian religions will be determined."

Prof. Hendrik Kraemer, in his book *The Christian Message in a Non-Christian World*, summed up the issue involved in the situation of the Christian movement in China in the following words:

There is one point of crucial importance to be kept in mind in regard to China. Nobody will deny that China will be one of the classic places in the world where Christianity and Humanism will have their second eventful encounter (the first being that with Greek and Roman Humanism). . . . . The natural way for Christianity to become indigenous in China and remain at the same time truly Christian, is to relate itself to the fundamental apprehensions of Chinese culture by a process of mutual attraction and repulsion, just as the Church went through a similar experience in the first centuries of its existence in regard to its Greek-Roman-Oriental environment.[11]

Paradoxical as it may seem, China will understand Christianity more quickly and more easily if Christianity will seek to understand China and China's religious heritage and traditions more fully and more deeply. This is one of the great problems and tasks of missions, which, if successfully undertaken, will not only greatly facilitate and accelerate the advancement of the Christian move-

[11] Harper & Brothers, 1938, pp. 385-86.

34

ment in China, but will also be a significant factor and an important contribution to the building up of a more and more Christianized world community, upon which world harmony and the happiness of mankind so much depend.

II. RELIGIOUS BACKGROUND AND BASIC BELIEFS OF THE CHINESE

In religion, as perhaps in many other things, China sometimes appears to be an Oriental puzzle which cannot be easily explained or analyzed. To start with, we do not exactly know whether to say that the Chinese are very religious or very little religious. Comparing them with some of the outstanding religious people of the world, we have to say that religion has not played so prominent a part in their national life as, for instance, in the case of the Jews, the Hindus, and the Mohammedans. As compared with Western countries, we may say that from some points of view they have more religion in their daily life than is the case in an average Christian community of the West; but from some other points of view they are quite indifferent: for example, they have never had an Established Church or a national religion in the Western sense of the term, nor have they ever actually fought over the question of religion.

35

In their religious life and ideas we find some of the most ridiculous superstitions existing side by side with the most exalted moral ideals. If, however, they are not intensely religious, they are at least genuinely moral; if they are not spiritual, they are at least ethical; if they have not been taught that their first devotion is to serve God, they have at least been instructed that their chief pursuit in life is not to worship mammon; if theology does not particularly attract their attention, a certain idealism at least is part of their mental make-up.

Two things may be said by way of preliminary remark. First, in a land where there is the greatest single aggregation of people, and where for ages three religions—and now five—have been active in force, and where therefore we would not be surprised if there were the widest range of religious ideas and the greatest diversity of religious practices, we find that, in spite of all, there is sufficient harmony of thought and faith to make the vast people homogeneous. Secondly, whereas for a long time in many countries the church predominated and controlled education, in China it has always been the scholar who has dominated the religious thought of the nation. In other words, in Western countries the clergy or priest took on the function of the scholar and educator, while in China the scholar did much of the work of the priest in developing the religious thought of the people.

What are some of the essential features and general characteristics of the religious life of the Chinese people?

The first interesting thing which we will notice in the religious life of the Chinese is that it is eclectic and not dogmatic. Eclecticism is perhaps its most dominant, as well as its most interesting, characteristic. It is at once the most ridiculous and the most sensible. Instead of acting like a blind man holding on to the tusk or the trunk or the leg or the tail of an elephant, and insisting that he thereby knows how the whole elephant looks, the Chinese observer starts with the admission that his vision is limited and imperfect, that he may be color-blind or may have blind spots in the eyes so that he cannot see clearly and perfectly the whole elephant all at once. He is therefore willing to have different parties see the same elephant from different points of view, and then have them compare notes with each other, and thus get a more composite and perhaps a more correct picture of the whole.

China is traditionally spoken of as "a land of three religions." Confucianism, Taoism, and Buddhism have long lived side by side, not entirely without rivalry or friction, but, on the whole,

37

peacefully and amicably. The Chinese adherents of these three systems have shown that, even in the realm of religion, where fanatic enthusiasm has produced some of the fiercest wars of human history, they could actually live for centuries on the principle of live and let live, preferring, shall we say, the Virginia reel to a punch in the ring. Not that they were indifferent to any distinction between truth and falsehood; but they never did believe that force alone could effect any deep or permanent change in man's attitude, and they had faith to believe that time would prove all things. In China we often say that a paper tiger cannot stand the wear and tear of life's vicissitude, but that pure gold will become purer and brighter if put through the test of fire.

The most interesting point in this situation has been the matter-of-fact attitude of the people toward it. It seemed to be so natural that no particular explanations were called for. The Chinese people have often said that every religion aims at teaching man to be good. Any religion is better than none. Different men have different tastes; and different constitutions require different vitamins.

There is, however, another interesting fact in this situation which deserves particular mention, namely, that there is essential unity amidst the apparent diversity. While there are religious adherents designated as Confucianists, Buddhists, and Taoists, it is not far from truth to say that all Chinese are basically Confucianists, though some have an additional or particular leaning toward Buddhism or Taoism.

Explanations for this eclecticism may be found both in the nature of these three religions and in the temperament and psychology of the Chinese people.

As to the nature of these religions, it will not be difficult to see that they are not mutually exclusive, but rather mutually supplementary. Confucianism, with its emphasis on the practical problems of life, leaves plenty of room for the mysticism of Taoism on the one hand and for the metaphysics of Buddhism on the other.

For an explanation of the eclecticism in the temperament and psychology of the Chinese people, the following may be mentioned:

1. Chinese philosophy teaches that the field of knowledge is unlimited in extent, so that no man nor any age can claim to comprehend the whole truth. To learn from all persons at all times is the pathway to wisdom. Confucius said, "In any company of three one would find a teacher, and could take the good for an example, and the bad for a warning." [12] That attitude of the humble learner

[12] Analects iii. 21.

39

is typical of the spirit of learning. It has also been said in China that only the river bed which is low enough to absorb hundreds of small streams flowing into it can become a river of mighty waters.

2. Chinese philosophy teaches the unity and universality of truth. One truth and another truth put together make more truth and not less truth. Truth is truth wherever found—in Buddhism, or in Taoism, or anywhere else. The Chinese would not be apt to say, "Can anything good come out of Nazareth?" Chinese classics therefore often speak of arriving at the same destination by different routes, and coming to the same conclusion through different ways of thinking.

3. The Chinese are, by teaching and in temperament, moderate and tolerant. A gentleman never fights, and a wise man does not argue with anybody upon whom reason is not likely to prevail. Everybody can air his own views, but the truth will ultimately vindicate itself.

The second general characteristic we can mention is that the religion of China is humanistic and not theological. To the Chinese, religion is not so much a subject for philosophical speculation as it is a matter for practical application. The essential purpose and function of religion is not to try to know the unknowable or explain the inexplicable, not to trace the origin of the universe and explore the mysteries of life; but to formulate rules and to set down principles for dealing with life as it is, in order to make it richer and nobler. Religion is for life, and not life for religion.

Religion for the Chinese is not theology about a Supreme God, but morality concerning one's fellow men. China has not produced any great theologian who set his heart on trying to understand the attributes of Deity or the genesis of the universe. In China there have been many moral philosophers who have centered their discussions on human nature, whether originally good or originally evil; but it was always with a view to finding the correct way for moral improvement and development. There have been, of course, interesting myths and legends about the gods and the creation; but they were taken just as myths and no more, and nobody paid very serious attention to them as an accurate account of what had actually happened. It was assumed that the world must have had a beginning, and that in the beginning there must have been a Creator. But there was nobody to witness the creation, and so there could be no really authentic account. One person's guess is perhaps almost as good as that of another. Chinese philosophy has given a good place to intuitive perception, but has had no room for direct revelation. The center of the world of thought, as

41

well as the world of life, has been man and this life of his. God is not ignored, but no attempt has been made to lift the veil of mystery in which his nature and attributes are shrouded. The religion of the Chinese is from man to God, rather than from God to man.

Because Chinese religion is humanistic, it is also intensely practical. Theories in the abstract were but form without substance and not held in high esteem. *Tao* (truth) and *Teh* (virtue) were always mentioned together and often used as a compound noun. So, truth must become virtue. Word must become flesh. "Knowledge and conduct must be united into one," said Wang Yang-ming, one of the best known of the more modern Confucian scholars who lived several hundred years ago.

The term, Heavenly Father, of course did not exist in the old Chinese concept. Yet, curiously enough, the component parts, "Heaven" and "Father," have been terms most frequently used in expressing two of the most fundamental concepts in Chinese religion and philosophy. Heaven is the supreme power above; father is the chief authority below. Either was frequently thought of in terms of the other by analogy. To say that "heaven" is man's father above, and that father is man's "heaven" or god below, will not be an altogether far-fetched simile or a too unnatural comparison.

42

Yet a third characteristic of the religious life of the Chinese is that his religion is both communal and personal. We can conceive of his religion divided up, like the Temple of the Old Testament, into the outer court and the inner sanctuary. If China is a land of three religions, we can say that the Chinese individual is a man of two religions. There is a public side to his religion which is a part of good citizenship. This includes religious ceremonies which he observes as a community obligation, centering in the family and society. This is the part which he goes through in form, without entering into in spirit. He does it, not necessarily because he believes in it, but because he feels that he belongs to it. This is his social obligation in religion, which he carries out because of social etiquette; and good manners call everywhere for a man when in Rome to do as the Romans do.

But in addition to this superficial life there is yet another side to his religious life which is born of his own faith, and which is a part of his own inner life. This is his real religion. This is his "holy of holies," where he really meets his god, and where he worships in spirit and in truth. It is for this reason perhaps that a Chinese can be both a Confucianist and a Buddhist without any sense of contradiction or incongruity.

His real religion is strictly private and personal.

43

It is his personal relationship with the Divine. His devotion is carried on essentially in solitary meditation and private worship, and is expressed in earnest self-culture and in good moral conduct. This has two implications. It is a region wherein nobody should interfere; but it is also a place where he does not, as a rule, share the roof with anybody else. So, congregational worship, except as a family affair on certain special occasions, does not exist. Even when we find a temple thronged with crowds of people, they all act as individuals, each making his own prayer, and burning his own incense. Church affiliation and congregational worship are distinctly Christian institutions, and innovations in Chinese religious life. Often, therefore, the idea of church relationship is detached from Christian belief. Consequently, there are persons in China—how many it is difficult to say—who are pretty thoroughly Christian in belief and in spirit, but who, nevertheless, for one reason or another, do not join the church. In this, however, we perhaps find one explanation why the church membership remains so small when the Christian influence in the country is now so markedly strong.

A fourth characteristic of religion in China is the fact that it is integral and not compartmental. Religion is an integral part of the whole training for life, rather than just the central compartment or the top floor of the structure of life. Religion is substantially identified with morality; and morality is an integral part of educational culture. We may say that, to the Chinese, education, morality, and religion are inseparably linked together; they are the three legs which together form one triangle. Theoretically, there cannot be such a thing as a man of education who is a moral delinquent. There is a presumption of nobleness in the educated. It is, of course, only prima-facie evidence, easily refutable by actual facts. But under the old regime, when corporal punishment in open court was permitted, no magistrate could so disgrace a scholar who had won a degree under the old examination system without first disqualifying him as degree-holder. Actually, if a man's character was notoriously bad, he was perhaps never regarded as a member of the literati or intelligentsia,[13] no

[13] This was a very interesting body. There was no formal organization—no "bar examination" for admission; no "Phi Beta Kappa key" as a distinguishing badge; no stated meetings, except that they gathered together twice a year at the Confucian temples for the spring and autumn sacrifices; no definite system of ostracizing a member for unbecoming conduct. Yet, it was a body whose voice, when it did speak, could speak with an authority carrying more weight in society than the words of a district magistrate. A pronouncement "ex cathedra" of a mass meeting of the literati would be looked upon as the final verdict in the supreme court of intelligent opinion and moral consciousness.

45

matter how brilliant an intellectual genius he might be.

To be called a scholar, a man must have the good conduct worthy of his calling. In fact, learning is for virtue first, and for knowledge second. Although not in exactly these words, the Chinese believe that the fear of God is the beginning of wisdom. The first lesson of life is to know the moral of life. The Confucian conception of education is not only the training of the intellect but the development of the man; so in the Book of Great Learning the definition of education started with "to elucidate (through knowledge) or illustrate (through life) illustrious virtue."

This moral emphasis on education could perhaps be illustrated by what was my first lesson in Chinese. On my first day in school I was given five Chinese characters written on five sheets of square red paper. They were the Chinese words for heaven, earth, king, parents, and teacher. In these five characters we learned on the very first day of our schooling we would get an idea, an impression of growing vividness and significance as we moved on more and more to mature understanding in later life, that a man's fundamental relations are these: with heaven and earth, which conveyed the idea of God; with the king, who is the symbolic representative of the state and community; with the parents, who head the whole family system; with the teacher, who stands *in loco parentis*, because he is the one who gives us intellectual and spiritual birth.

This significance became more apparent when compared with what I learned from an English primer when I first started to study that language:

> One, one, one, a little dog run,
> Two, two, two, two cats see you,
> Three, three, three, three birds on a tree,
> Four, four, four, four rats on a floor.

How intensely practical was the one, and how significantly idealistic the other. Here we find facts and science versus ideals and philosophy. Could a young child appreciate what he was learning on his first day in school? No, certainly not at that time! But he would always remember what were the first characters he learned and would gradually understand why it was done.

Turning now from the religious life of the Chinese people, let us examine some of their basic religious beliefs.

To start with, we may say that the Chinese have always believed in a God. In view of the fact that Confucius had very little to say about future life and refrained from discussing gods and supernatural beings, and that many forms of animistic worship still prevail, there is perhaps a popular misconcep-

47

tion that the Chinese are atheistic or animistic in their belief about God. The fact of the matter is that the Chinese are theistic and, essentially speaking, monotheistic—at least in the sense that they have always believed in the existence of a Supreme Ruler of the universe. There was no more fundamental belief with the Chinese than their belief that God is—that he lives and rules, and that he sees and cares.

Atheism now exists in China; but it is a part of the "new learning," introduced from the West, rather than a part of the religious heritage which has come down from the past. God may be called by different names, such as, Providence, Heaven, Supreme Ruler, *Shang Ti*, etc.; his nature and attributes may not be well known; but that there is in the universe a supreme controlling power, which is intelligent, moral, and benevolent, has always been accepted without question. God or Heaven is the ultimate standard of our reference, the supreme objective of our reverence, and the postulate upon which the whole theory of life was built. The traditional definition of man who is hopelessly lost is that he is a man who fears neither Heaven nor Earth.

Next to the belief in God, we may mention, as the basic belief of the Chinese, their faith that the world is a moral order. They have implicit con-

48

fidence in the ultimate triumph of reason over force, and of righteousness over wickedness. An often-quoted Chinese proverb says that "that which is in accord with Heaven prospers, and that which is against Heaven will perish." If the wicked prosper and the good suffer, it is not because the moral law of just reward fails to work, but because the time of reckoning has not yet come. Watchful waiting, not hopeless despair, is the typical Chinese attitude. The immutable law of cause and effect in the moral realm is considered as certain as the fact that water will seek its own level. Even as Paul taught in Galatians 6:7, "Whatsoever a man soweth, that shall he also reap," in due course in one form or another. If Heaven does not reward or punish a person directly or immediately, it will surely come upon his children or children's children.

Because of this implicit faith in a dependable moral order in the world, the Chinese always put their trust in the final supremacy of virtue and in the eventual downfall of any order of force. If they are superstitious, one of their outstanding "superstitions" is their unshaken belief that virtue exalts a nation, and is the only reliable and permanent stabilizing force in the world, while an order resting on force is in a perpetual state of unstable equilibrium. For this faith the Chinese have at times paid heavily; yet I hope they will hold on to this belief, giving it perhaps a more realistic interpretation and protecting it, at the same time, with the necessary practical safeguards.

So much importance is attached to this idea of virtue, and so deep is the conviction that virtue must come out on top in the long run, that, just as there can hardly be a successful play on the occidental stage without a love story, so there cannot be a popular play on the Chinese stage without a moral in it—usually on one of the four topics, patriotism, filial piety, conjugal faithfulness, or loyalty among friends. In all classical shows not modified by modern dramatic ideals, success and virtue must embrace and kiss each other when the curtain falls.

Their faith that the world is a moral order is perhaps due to a third basic belief of the Chinese, namely, their conviction of the excellence and permanence of the spiritual values of life. Knowledge or learning is divided into two categories: that which is above form (spiritual things), and that which is below form or with form (material things). All men are busy and eager for something in life. The difference between the superior man and the inferior man is that the former diligently seeks after truth and righteousness, while the latter eagerly goes after gains. In China it is most popular for a man to describe himself as the "shivering scholar," that is, one who is poor in material possessions but rich in spiritual gifts of a brilliant intellect and noble virtues; one who is not clad in gorgeous robes but clothed in beauty of character. The teaching that the *Chun Tze* (princely man or superior man) should set his heart on truth and righteousness (*Tao*), and should look upon wealth and honor as fleeting clouds, has been so emphasized in the development of the ideal personality of the Chinese that the spiritual values of life have always been considered the more excellent portion. Here again the Chinese have suffered because of their conviction. Here again the ideals may have to be readjusted. The neglect of material civilization and material progress should be duly corrected; but the center of gravity, I hope, will not be radically shifted away from the traditional emphasis on spiritual values.

Such are some of the more outstanding features of the religious background of the Chinese people. It appears that in their fundamental philosophy of life they have been much influenced by at least three things—humanism, rationalism, and idealism. Because they are humanistic, they have always centered their thought upon the possibilities of man and the welfare of mankind. Because they are rationalistic, they have always kept up their faith in the supremacy and ultimate triumph of reason over force. Because they are idealistic, they have always been taught to value spiritual qualities more than physical properties.

To the theologians and religious philosophers these are perhaps not qualities of distinct religious significance. But do we not find in them some elements of true worth and permanent value? Does not the cultural heritage of the Chinese make them responsive to the appeal of a rational, dynamic religion? And finally, shall we not say that the basic moral philosophy of the Chinese seems to be more in line with than in opposition to the Christian ideals of life, and that the world of ideals in which the Chinese have been living is not too far away from the Christian conception of society?

In the Book of Genesis it was said that "the Lord God formed man of the dust of the ground, and breathed into his nostrils the breath of life; and man became a living soul." The model of ideal manhood which Chinese moral and religious philosophy has set up is indeed only an earthly figure, yet has it not been so fashioned that with the breath of God making it a living soul it can be transformed into a being which can be developed "unto a perfect man, unto the measure of the stature of the fulness of Christ"? Are we not even tempted to say that it seems almost natural and logical to expect that eventually the Christian of the West will find in this gentleman of the East a congenial companion, embracing the same faith, following the same Master, and co-operating as an apostle on the same mission? Is this not a stimulating thought and a challenging idea?

II

CONFUCIANISM:
THE ART OF LIVING

I. CONFUCIUS, THE GREAT TEACHER
OF THE CHINESE

Confucius is both the national symbol and the national model as we think of China and the Chinese. He is the outstanding "father Jacob" of the Chinese nation.

One of the most interesting spots in the Capitol Building in Washington, D. C., is the Statuary Hall, to which each state of the United States of America is invited to send in two statues of its most distinguished citizens. If ever there should be a hall of immortals in the "parliament of man," to which each member of a world federation may send in two statues, one of these from China would surely be a statue of Confucius.

For nearly twenty-five centuries Confucius has been the life companion and life guide of the Chinese people. He has marched at the head of the procession in their long, unbroken trek down the road of history as their honored teacher and spiritual leader. He has long lived in the thought and imagination of the Chinese people, unfolding before their eyes a noble vision of life, speaking to their ears inspiring words of wisdom, and stirring up in their hearts lofty aspirations and high ideals. To his influence Chinese society is much indebted for its practical outlook, broad vision, and its moral tone, as well as its harmony and stability. The system of teachings which bears his name has been the most potent single factor in shaping the life and character of the entire Chinese people; and it has succeeded in molding them into one homogeneous unity.

For a while, in the early days of the Chinese Republic, Confucius was temporarily eclipsed; his glory waned and the lights were dimmed. Along with the other dignitaries of the old regime, he was shown the door of exit. But while most of the others remained shut outside, old man Confucius was soon invited back, and again given a seat of honor.

Although the attempt to create a state religion out of Confucianism failed in the constitutional convention in the early days of the Chinese Republic, nevertheless Confucius' birthday is now observed as Teacher's Day. He is thus identified with the most honored and most influential profession in the country. He therefore still has excellent connections. At the same time, it also shows in what high esteem the teacher is held in China.

Today Confucianism is far from being discarded or becoming obsolete in China. It is not a back number on the shelf of culture, which will no longer be touched. It no longer has the predominant influence it once had, but it will continue to be a strong influence and a living factor. Its teachings, of course, will have to be re-evaluated and reinterpreted in the new light which mankind has seen since the days of Confucius, and in terms of the conditions of the living present, by the "modern critics" among Confucian scholars.

Both the continuing influence of classical moral ideals and the process of their re-evaluation and reinterpretation in the new light of modern conditions were admirably illustrated in the New Life Movement, which was started in China in 1934. In form, the call of the New Life Movement was for a return to China's traditional emphasis upon morality and virtue, particularly to a rededication of individual and national life to the time-honored principles of *Li, Yi, Lien, Chu*—propriety, righteousness, honesty, and conscientiousness (i.e., a keen sense of shame for any failure of proper moral conduct). In its spirit and outlook, no Christian can think of this New Life Movement without thinking of the words of the Master to Nicodemus: "Except a man be born again, he cannot see the kingdom of God." It was, in a way, just a movement to revive and reinvigorate certain time-honored old moral precepts, but in it we certainly also see distinct manifestations of new ideas and a new spirit. While it was not a Christian Movement, it was thoroughly in accord with Christian spirit; in fact, the whole idea was born in the minds of two great Christians in China.

II. What Is Confucianism?

Confucianism is nominally the teachings of Confucius, the great sage of China. But actually and in a larger sense it includes the whole system of the moral-political-religious philosophy of the Chinese which was summed up by Confucius, and which was carried on and developed by his disciples and later scholars.

Confucius was naturally and appropriately the central figure in the system. But Confucius was not the whole of Confucianism. In fact, the traditional name for Confucianism was *Ju Chiao*, that is, "the teaching of the scholar" or "the cult of the cultured." It has always been so spoken of when used or referred to in connection with Buddhism and Taoism. Confucianism is the more modern name, which has come into vogue when used by

57

Western scholars in reference to, or in comparison with, Christianity.

Confucius did not claim for himself any final or exclusive authority to lay down a moral code or ethical system. He was a prophet. But he was not, and did not claim to be, the Prophet, like Mohammed, or the Christ, like Jesus. In his own words, "he was only a transmitter and not a maker, believing in and loving the ancients." [1] Confucius taught, and handed down, the truths coming from the ancient illustrious emperors *Yao* and *Shun;* and he made clear, and magnified, the systems established by the emperors *Wen* and *Wu*.[2]

Though Confucius was not a divine prophet, nevertheless he was a great teacher—the greatest in China, and one of the few really great teachers in the history of the world. He was also a very wise teacher, who taught the students how to learn as well as what to learn. His own method was indeed simply learning from the best in the past, and transmitting that rich heritage to the future. But in doing so he magnified and added to it in the process. He did more than just dig up the treasure hidden in the past; he improved it to some degree. What Confucius conceived to be a good teacher can be seen from this quotation: "He who

[1] Analects vii. 1.
[2] Doctrine of the Mean xxix.

58

can come to know the new, through reviewing the old, can be a teacher of others." [3] It was true wisdom because of its modesty; for most claims of entire originality were just foolishness. In his attainment, we find advancement rooted in continuity. There was progress and improvement, slow but sure, continuing and steady, conservatively and cautiously achieved. Things were not to remain static and stagnant. Make haste, but do it slowly.

III. Is Confucianism a Religion?

There is considerable divergence of opinion as to whether or not Confucianism is a religion. The question depends upon the definition of religion itself, on which there is a conspicuous lack of agreement. Some of the definitions are so vague that one does not know what one is grasping at; others, so intricate that one feels oneself lost in philosophical subtleties.

The only explicit definition or summary description of religion found in the Bible is: "Pure religion and undefiled before God and the Father is this, To visit the fatherless and widows in their affliction, and to keep himself unspotted from the world." [4] According to this functional characterization, Confucianism is a religion. For not only are

[3] Analects ii. 11.
[4] Jas. 1:27.

59

self-cultivation and personal character the essence of Confucian morality, but the care of the widow and the widower, the orphan and the childless, are considered as major social needs and the social concerns of a nation.[5]

If we should take the two essential elements of religion to be faith and worship, then we could say that Confucianism may be considered a religion with its major emphasis on faith and with only a minor emphasis on worship. As a faith, no religion has perhaps succeeded more than has Confucianism in knitting a whole nation together in a set of unquestioned beliefs—beliefs primarily concerning the practical rules of human conduct, but having their root in certain fundamental conceptions of an overruling Cosmic Order or Deity.

We may conclude by saying that Confucianism is not a religion in the fullest sense and according to the scientific definition of the term; but it is generally so considered, and it at least has functioned as a religion in China. Inasmuch as Confucianism, in its theological aspect, seeks a philosophical answer to the questions of the meaning of life and the purpose of living, and, in its practical aspect, the development of the individual and the improvement of society, it therefore certainly has an ob-

[5] Mencius, Bk. I. Pt. II. v. 3.

jective which is common to many religions. And may we not add that Confucianism has actually accomplished much of what the great religions of the world are seeking to accomplish, namely, peace on earth and good will among men.

IV. THE CENTRAL THEME OF CONFUCIANISM

The central theme of Confucianism is the *Art of Living*. It is chiefly concerned with the man as an individual living in social relations. It has very little or no interest in theorizing anthropologically about how man came into being, or speculating eschatologically on what happens to the individual when he ceases to be. All the teachings of Confucius, whether about rite or ceremony, benevolence or righteousness, have the same central objective in view, namely, to teach man how to live and what to live for: (1) living by himself, and (2) living with others.

The whole problem of life, in its concrete application, resolves itself into:

1. The development of the ideal man, the *Chun Tze*. This term may be best translated as the "princely man," although it is often rendered as the "superior man" or the "gentleman." This "princely man" is also the mature man, or the full-

grown man[6] (i.e., a man who is fully developed physically, intellectually, and morally), since his corresponding opposite is the "small or little man" (i.e., the child type, the immature or undeveloped man).

2. The building up of an ideal society. This is to be a kingdom of righteousness, wherein everybody fulfills his right function and maintains the right relationship; wherein "the king is kingly, the minister is 'ministerly,' the father is fatherly, and the son is sonly";[7] that is, wherein everybody, no matter who he is, or what he is, would, in all his relations, play the game of life according to the rules of life.

Ideal society can be realized only through the ideal man. Therefore, the main effort of Confucianism is the development, through education and moral cultivation, of the "princely man," who is the living cornerstone of the ideal society. Confucianism does not rest its case on law or government, ethical teaching or moral code, but ultimately upon good men—living personalities of sterling character. Any government or system continues to live and flourish when the man behind it is alive

[6] Perhaps similar to what Paul had in mind when he spoke of a man coming to the stature of the fulness of Jesus Christ in Ephesians 4:13.

[7] Analects xxii. 2.

and active; it dies and fades away when the man dies and disappears.[8] So, opposing the views of the Legalist School, Confucianism took the position that education rather than legislation is the bedrock for the foundation of good society. Prevention is always better than cure.

Confucianism is a one-word religion. The whole Confucian system of philosophy and morality can be summed up in the one simple Chinese word *Jen*, 仁 , which is a composite character made up of two simple characters, "man," 人 , and "two," 二 .

This word is frequently translated as "benevolence," because *Jen* is very often coupled with the word *Ai*, meaning "love," the two words forming the compound noun meaning "love and benevolence," or simply "love." But etymologically, and from various explanations and definitions given by Confucius, and as it was used in Confucian classics, it really has a broader meaning. So, a more correct and appropriate translation would be "altruism"; for the central idea there is the *alter ego*, the second man.

Jen is a person's proper attitude and proper relation toward the second man, the other fellow. This is the sum total of the Confucian teaching,

[8] Doctrine of the Mean xx. 2.

applicable both to the moral development of the individual and to the fundamental objective of social and political relations, in their national and also in their international aspects. Knowledge of life begins with the recognition of the *alter ego*, and ends with an adequate philosophy for dealing with this second man. So, at one place Confucius said, "The doctrine of *Jen* is the doctrine of man," [9] and at another place he said, "Benevolence is to love man, and knowledge is to know man." [10]

The Golden Rule is just the concrete application of this idea of *Jen:* the proper attitude toward, and relations with, the "second man." This, in Confucianism, is stated in the negative form: "Whatsoever ye do not desire that others should do unto you, do ye not even so to others." [11] As the beginning of moral consciousness is the recognition of the "second man," so the measure of morality is to deal with this "second man" (others) as you would deal with the "first man" (self). In other words, the measure of man is man; the standard for your attitude toward the "other selves" is your attitude—your hope, desire, and wants—toward your "own self." The whole problem of life has the "self" as Alpha and the "other self" as

[9] Doctrine of the Mean xx. 3.
[10] Analects xii. 22:1.
[11] Doctrine of the Mean xxiii. 3; *cf*. Analects xv. 23.

Omega—extending from the individual to the family, from the family to the nation, and from the nation to the world.

The universal moral law, stated in the simplest form, is, therefore, simply to push yourself into the position of the other. "If this is where you would like to stand, then let him stand here also; if there is where you would like to be, then let him be there also." [12]

Mencius read into or put into this negative form a very positive and social content when he said that we should "treat with due consideration and regard the aged ones of our own and extend the same to the aged of others; in the same way, treat the younger ones of our own and extend the same to the younger ones of others." [13]

This Confucian "golden rule" is often spoken of as the "silver rule," because it is stated in the negative form. The difference between the two, however, is essentially a difference in form, and not in spirit. The positive form is no doubt more perfect, being more dynamic; but Confucius was perhaps more concerned with laying down a practical rule of life than with the setting up of the highest ideal. In actual practice, we always start with the negative and proceed to the positive. We have to cease

[12] Analects vi. 23:2.
[13] Mencius, Bk. I. Pt. I. vii. 12.

to kill before we learn to love; we have to cease to covet before we start to give.

V. THE CONFUCIAN CLASSICS

The great source books of Confucianism are the "Five Classics" and the "Four Books." The former may be compared to the Old Testament portion of the Christian Bible, and the latter to the New Testament portion. As with the New Testament, so the "Four Books" are considered as having grown out of the antecedent scriptures and are much more familiar to the people.

The five canonical classics are:

1. Canon of History (*Shu King*)
2. Canon of Poetry (*Shih King*)
3. Canon of Changes (*I King*)
4. Record of Rites (*Li Ki*)
5. Annals of Spring and Autumn (*Chun Chiu*)

Of these five books, the Annals of Spring and Autumn was the only one written by Confucius. For the other four he only performed the task of an editor, gathering materials coming from ancient times, selecting those of permanent value for a "Reader's Digest."

The Canon of History is a collection of ancient historical documents which may be likened to the historical books of the Old Testament. The Canon of Poetry is a selection of about three hundred poems and folk songs out of many more which had come to the Chou Dynasty from ancient times. This may be likened to the Psalms. The Canon of Changes is a treatise on the sixty-four diagrams (permutations of six whole and six broken lines), a most mysterious book on which the Chinese theory of *Yin* and *Yang* was based and much used in divination. The Record of Rites is the "Book of Leviticus" in the Confucian classics. The Annals of Spring and Autumn reminds one of the Books of Chronicles in the Bible.

The "Four Books" are:

1. The Book of Great Learning (*Ta Hsueh*)
2. The Doctrine of the Mean (*Chung Yung*)
3. The Confucian Analects (*Lun Yu*)
4. The Works of Mencius (*Meng Tze*)

The following may serve as a very brief introduction to the main ideas in the "Four Books," which, in days before the introduction of the modern school system, every schoolboy had to commit to memory.

1. *The Book of Great Learning* (*Ta Hsueh*). The term *Ta Hsueh* is the designation now used in China for all universities. This book is a treatise on Higher Education and an essay on moral culture. Its central thought or thesis is succinctly

67

stated in the opening sentence. "The aim of Higher Education (or Great Learning) is to illuminate or illustrate the illustrious virtue, to renew or renovate the man, and to press on to the *summmum bonum.*" The Chinese phrase *Ming Ming Teh,* herein before translated "illustrate illustrious virtue," literally means "to brighten, bright (or shining) virtue." (The word *Ming* is a composite character made up of the two words for sun and moon.) "To brighten" carries both the idea of "to be enlightened"—that is, to have your mind so illuminated that you can see the truth—and "to enlighten or shine"—that is, to let your light so shine that truth may be glorified thereby. This is the true objective of real great learning or higher education. It starts with seeking to comprehend the truth and attains complete fulfillment when truth can be made to prevail in the whole world, or, as it is expressed in Chinese, to fill all space between heaven and earth. This is the *summmum bonum* which students of High Education, striving for Great Learning, must accept as their task and mission.

2. *The Doctrine of the Mean (Chung Yung).* This, the second of the "Four Books," contains some of the deepest, the most significant and beautiful ideas and ideals of Confucianism. It is a wonderful discourse on the Doctrine of the Golden

Mean, which has had profound influence upon the national character and temperament of the Chinese people. It may be said that the grand idea is the search for and the formulation of a statement of an eternal truth, or a rule of life, which can be of universal application.

According to the best accepted interpretation, given by the famous commentator *Chen Yi*, the Chinese word *Chung* (middle) means "not one-sided," and *Yung* (ordinary) means "constant" or "unchanging." In other words, *Chung Yung* means the constant, unchanging middle path, which is the golden mean between two extremes: excess and insufficiency. It calls for moderation and due degree. To go beyond misses the point, just as not going far enough. The golden mean is the proper center of gravity for all correct human actions.

As an illustration, when applying to the principle of benevolence, it condemns narrow selfishness, on the one hand, and disapproves uniform, undiscriminating love of all, on the other. It seeks to avoid both extremes and recommends "graded love." There is to be love for all, but there should be more for the nearest and dearest, and less for the unknown and unrelated—for example, naturally and rightly more for the father than for the stranger. In the application of love,

69

Confucianism does not go as far as Christianity, which exhorts all people to be as perfect in love as our Heavenly Father who makes the sun shine upon all men, good and evil alike; nor as far as Buddhism, which includes, besides human beings, animals, birds, and insects.

3. *The Analects* (*Lun Yu*). The Confucian Analects is a compilation of the discourses and sayings of Confucius and of dialogues with his disciples. This document is the principal source of our information on the life and ideals of this great sage of China. It occupies a place in the Confucian classics comparable with the Gospels in the Bible. Its universal familiarity to the intelligentsia or literati of China has given to the Chinese people a great common denominator in their thought and ideals, which goes a long way to explain the homogeneity of the Chinese people.

It was not written by one author or at one time. It consists of chapters and articles only loosely grouped together without any particular purpose in arrangement. It is a synopsis of the "Confucian Gospels," but not arranged in any chronological order nor grouped together according to the authors.

It covers, of course, a wide range of subjects dealing with ethics and morality as they apply to the individual, the family, the society, and the state or government. If there is one topic which can be regarded as the cornerstone around which all other parts of the structure fit together it is the Master's discourse and description of the *Chun Tze*, the ideal man.

4. *The Works of Mencius* (*Meng Tze*). Mencius is to Confucianism what Paul is to Christianity. The Book or Books of Mencius can be compared to the Epistles of Paul in the Bible. The sayings of Mencius are written in a much more vigorous style than are the recorded sayings of Confucius. Though he started with the same fundamental conceptions that Confucius did, and encouraged the same virtues, Mencius seemed to be much more socially and politically minded. While both of them looked forward to an ideal society, we may draw a distinction by saying that Confucius talked more about the *Chun Tze*, the "princely man," whereas Mencius discussed more the *Huang Tao*, the "kingly way" of government, and thus emphasized more than his great master the idea of the social and political gospel in Confucianism.

The two most favorite themes of Mencius are (1) benevolence and righteousness in government and (2) the inherent goodness of human nature. The one is the basis of good government, and the other is the starting point of the moral develop-

71

ment of the individual. The impression which Mencius left upon China in both of these two respects has been deep and lasting.

In the Confucian Analects we get a picture of a great sage, sublime and serene, firm yet gentle, dispensing words of practical wisdom. In the works of Mencius we see an ardent reformer, with dynamic convictions and a ringing message, who typified the hero in action and who personified the "grand air" of righteous enthusiasm.

VI. Specific Teachings of Confucianism

1. *On God and Religion.* Confucius did not indulge in the philosophical and theological discussion about deity and religion. Confucius was devout but not religious, if such distinction is possible.

The *raison d'être* for this attitude can be surmised from some of his well-known remarks. "If you know not life, why speculate about (life after) death." [14] That is to say, you have sufficient to engage your attention with the problems of the present life; do not sidetrack them with guesses about a future life concerning which a man can only surmise. The orderly, logical process is "to proceed from the low to the high, and to go from the near to the far." [15] Do not try to run before

[14] Analects ix. 11:1.
[15] Doctrine of the Mean xiv. 1.

72

you know how to walk. And is it not intellectual honesty "to claim as knowledge only what you do know and to admit that you do not know what you don't know"? [16] Confucius was homocentric and practical, interested more in concrete rules of living than in speculative philosophy of life. Whatever religion he had was from man to God, and not from God to man.

However, in refraining from discussing deity and future life Confucius simply admitted his own intellectual limitations; he did not thereby deny anything, either concerning the existence of God or the fact of future life. Confucius was not at all atheistic. Not only did he recognize the existence of a Supreme Deity of the universe, whom he sometimes referred to as "Heaven" (*Tien*) and sometimes as the "Supreme Ruler" (*Shang Ti*), but he took it for granted that everybody would agree with him on this point, and made it the basis of his whole structure of philosophy without argumentation.

This "Heaven" or "Supreme Ruler" is not a mere abstract concept or a blind force of nature. It is a conscious being and a personality, omniscient and omnipotent, moral and benevolent, keenly interested in human welfare. It is not merely some god who sits high up in the heaven of

[16] Analects i. 17.

heavens, remote and removed from the world, but one who is touched with the needs of man, and who is vitally interested in the moral order of the world. Heaven's care and concern are always the interest and happiness of "my people."

Man's attitude toward God is essentially one of reverence and respect, rather than one of love. It was "respect for Heaven" rather than love for God which Confucius considered the proper religious attitude for man to have. The conception lacks the warmth of the Christian conception of God as our Heavenly Father, but it also keeps man from presuming so much on the loving nature of God as to run the risk of becoming "naughty children." To the Chinese, the Supreme Deity is a just and holy God rather than a loving and forgiving Father. Respect, and not love, is the attitude and the sentiment most emphasized among the Chinese people—not only in religion but also in human relations.

Yet, we must say that Confucius claimed no divine origin either for himself or for his teaching. We can well imagine that he felt, along with other ancient worthies, that he had a sort of divine commission in life. Nevertheless, he was just a man doing a man's job. Although the disciples of Confucius referred to him as the "rousing bell of Heaven," essentially he spoke as man to man. In this respect Confucianism has been more consistent than

Buddhism, for, although Buddha also spoke as man to man, it was not long before his disciples turned him into a god among the gods.

Confucius did not even claim that he was a perfect man; in fact, the spirit which he wanted his disciples to catch was his sense of humility and regret that he had fallen so short of his ideals and must therefore make more earnest efforts. He was just a humble and indefatigable traveler on the path of truth and righteousness, eagerly and steadfastly pressing on with a fixed purpose. In one thing only he claimed to excel others: namely, in his keenness and eagerness to learn and forever to keep on learning—to respect Heaven and serve men. In the profound, universal respect of the Chinese for education and culture, and in the diligence and earnestness of the students, we see something of the impression which Confucius has made upon the Chinese through the influence of his personality.

2. *On Man and His Moral Development*. Man is the prime subject of Confucianism. The development of man and the improvement of human society in its ever-widening circles are its sole aim and effort.

What are the postulates or fundamental assumptions of Confucius concerning man—his nature and development? First, while he does not speak of an *imago dei* in the human personality, orthodox Con-

75

fucianism does affirm that all men are endowed with
a good nature by Heaven. Thus the *Chung Yung*,
the Book of the Doctrine of the Golden Mean,
defines nature as that which is endowed or ordered
by Heaven. Both Mencius and *Chu Hsi*, the best
exponent of Neo-Confucianism, stressed the point
that man's original nature is good. The latter as-
serted that the whole trouble with man's moral life
is that his good self is like a clean mirror covered
by dust, and all that is needed is to dust it off.
Secondly, all men are educable and all can climb
up on the rungs of the ladder of education. There
are of course different groups in society, but
through self-effort and education man can cross
from one group or one social stratum to another,
and thus he is able to rise from the humblest beginning to the highest possibility in life. Thirdly,
it follows as a necessary corollary that all men are
essentially or fundamentally alike. This in turn
means that in their spiritual development they all
have the capacity to be as *Yao* and *Shun* (two legendary kings who were also models of virtue),
and in their social relations men are "all brothers
within the four seas." "*Ssu Hai Chih Nei Chieh
Hsiung Ti Yeh*." [17] Indeed, "A man's a man for
a' that!" in his intrinsic worth and moral pos-

[17] Analects xii. 5:4.

sibilities, whether he comes from the East or the West, the North or the South.

Man gets wiser through learning, and better through the practice of virtue. The Confucian theory of moral development may be described as the "theory of concentric ever-widening circles." There are four or eight steps involved, depending upon whether we start with the action or conduct of the individual or go behind the conduct and action to the spring of thought and knowledge. The first set of four steps we may call "morality in action"; and the second set of four steps we may call "morality in cultivation."

The four progressive steps in "morality in action" are self-cultivation (or pruning the self), ordering the family, governing the country, and harmonizing the world. The word used in this last connection is very significant. It is the word *Ping*, which means to level, to equalize, or to even up— for example, to bring the underprivileged as nearly as possible up to the level of the privileged, and to even up, in some way, the "haves" and the "have-nots." It is very significant that Confucianism speaks of governing a country, but it does not speak of governing the world. It speaks of equalizing, or "equity-lizing," all that which is under heaven (*Ping Tien Hsia*). It cherishes no dream of world

77

empire, but it does envision universal peace and harmony.

The procedure herein suggested may be illustrated by a diagram of a series of concentric ever-widening circles, starting from a moral self, passing to a moral family, then to a moral nation, and finally to a moral world. It also makes three other suggestions as practical measures in aid of moral development: to draw carefully the distinction between the fundamentals and incidentals of life; to follow a proper order of sequence, that is, by giving first attention to things of first importance; and to have a due sense of proportion.

As in "morality in action," so in "morality in cultivation," there are also four progressive steps—investigation of things, knowledge of the final objective, rectification of the heart, sincerity of purpose. The list represents four fundamental procedures, namely, to study, to know, to will, and to do. Here we have another series of four concentric circles. The proposition that moral culture should start with the investigation of things, has been a puzzle to many thinkers. But here of course the word "thing" refers to both material and immaterial objects—nature, phenomena, material things, spiritual values, life forms, and life ideals. Investigation is necessary to determine qualities and appraise values. Its full significance can perhaps

78

be more easily seen when we consider this along with another principle, which appears to be rather inconsequential but which Confucius insisted upon as being supremely important, namely, the rectification of names—the importance of true classification and proper definitions. Why should a matter of names be so important? Well, the answer is that it is important to distinguish clearly that black is black, and white is white. One must call good, good, and bad, bad, each by its proper name. This cannot be done, and definitions will not be accurate, until and unless one has made, in a thoroughgoing scientific way, a careful investigation and designation of all things.

3. *On Society and Its Aims*. The glorious vision which Confucius and his disciples set before the people of China is an ideal society in this world. This, however, is not a Kingdom of God on the principle of love, but a kingdom of man on the principle of righteousness. Love has its place in the system, but it is only to be the salt with which righteousness is to be seasoned. Someone once asked Confucius, "What do you say concerning the principle that injury should be recompensed with kindness?" The Master said: "With what then will you recompense kindness? Recompense injury with justice, and recompense kindness with kindness." To the vast majority of people who

79

have neither treated you with particular kindness nor have done you particular injury, is it not right to treat them with benevolence—that is, to be kindly disposed to them in love, but not ignoring the requirements of justice, so that righteousness may be maintained?

According to Confucianism this righteousness can be best secured through moral instruction and influence directed to the promotion and preservation of right relations among individuals and social units in the world. Right relations involve the development of the right kind of persons maintaining the right kind of attitudes toward other persons. Hence the emphasis on the clear understanding and careful observance of human relations in society. If the great objective of Western social and political science is the promotion and protection of human interests, that of Confucian philosophy is the adjustment of human relations. The whole social machine will run smoothly if the individuals in and the component parts of society are all nicely fitted into each other, in perfect gear and running order.

While *Jen* is declared to be the root and measure of all virtues in human relations, in order to be more explicit and specific we have laid down for us the five cardinal virtues to which we should particularly pay attention. These are *Jen* or

Benevolence, *Yi* or Righteousness, *Li* or Propriety, *Chih* or Wisdom, and *Hsin* or Fidelity, that is, faith and faithfulness. The first three belong to the realm of theory, and the second two belong to the realm of action. The first three are objects to be comprehended, and the second two are objects to be demonstrated or practiced in conduct.

The relationship of the first three can perhaps be best explained by using a tree as an analogy. *Jen* or Benevolence (in the larger Confucian sense) is the root of all moral, good and proper, action. *Yi* or Righteousness is the trunk of the tree, the manifestations of *Jen* in its applications to life and living. *Li* or rules of Propriety (including etiquette and ceremony but larger than both) are the various branches of the trunk, or the concrete detailed rules of conduct based upon the idea of Righteousness which springs from Benevolence (comparable to the laws of the Pharisees). *Chih* or Wisdom is the apprehension of Truth. *Hsin* or Fidelity is faith and faithfulness in the application of the knowledge of Truth thus apprehended. If we should continue further the use of the figure of the tree, we could say that Wisdom is the flower, and Faith the fruit, on this tree of virtue.

Confucianism recognizes five fundamental relations in society. These are those between sovereign and minister (or between the state and the citizen),

81

between father and son, between husband and wife, between elder brother and younger brother, and between friends.[18]   Between father and son there should be family affection; between sovereign and minister, righteousness; between husband and wife, differentiation of functions (or division of labor); between elder brother and younger brother, a proper order of precedence; between friends, fidelity.[19]   These five relations probably do not exhaust the whole range of a person's political, family, and social obligations, but are they not the most fundamental? and are not the principles mentioned in connection with them truly basic?   The importance attached to family relations in Chinese society is well known to the West, but the relationship between friends is equally important, though less known.   The Chinese conception of the value and importance of friendship is well reflected in the popular proverb, "When at home rely upon your parents; when away from home depend upon your friends."

These five fundamental relations involve ten different parties, giving rise to ten different principles or attitudes which, by analogy, may be called the "ten commandments of Confucian philosophy." These ten principles, as stated in the classics, are

[18] Doctrine of the Mean xx. 8.
[19] Mencius, Bk. III. Pt. I. iv. 8.

82

that the father should be kind; the son, filial; the elder brother, good; the younger brother, respectful; the husband, righteous; the wife, listening; the elder, gracious; the junior, complaisant; the ruler or king, benevolent (*Jen*); the subjects or officials, loyal.

Two very interesting characteristics of these human relationships, as set forth in Confucianism, deserve special mention. First, all these relations deal with duties and obligations, and not rights and interests. It is not a question of what a person can hopefully expect from others, but the question of what he should rightfully do to others. Each is taught to be careful with regard to the beam in his own eye and not the mote in the eye of the other person. Secondly, all these obligations are relative, and not absolute; they are bilateral, and not unilateral; they are correlated and co-ordinated, reciprocal and not one-sided. While emphasis is primarily placed upon each person doing what he ought to do, there are imaginable circumstances when gross violation of the obligations by one party would modify or even absolve the other party from carrying out his corresponding obligation. This is a point particularly stressed by Mencius in discussing the reciprocal relationship between the ruler and his subjects.

4. *On the Family*. The basic unit in the Con-

fucian social structure is the family. The individual is not ignored, but he operates from the "home base." In fact, all human relations, even those in the political state and in the realm of religion, are expressed in terms of the family relationship.

There is a practical reason for this. Confucianism regards the family as the logical starting point for moral development. It requires little persuasion for a man to apply the principles of benevolence and due regard for others to members of his own family. It is by learning the lessons well in family circles that he can be taught, in degrees and by successive steps, to extend them to the community, to the nation, and, finally, to the world at large. When these good moral sentiments of love and due regard for others can be extended to members of the community, then will we have the right kind of society; when applied by the ruler in dealing with his subjects, then will we have the proper form of government; when extended to the world, then will we have a real, happy family of nations. But, for all this extensive achievement in promoting civic virtues and world citizenship, the home is to be the training school and experimental station.

It must thus be clear that this emphasis upon the home is not to make it an end in itself, but to make use of it as a means to an end. Attention is centered on the home because the home is to be the training center for moral cultivation in the development of social and public virtues. Filial piety is to be regarded as the greatest virtue not only because it is right that we should remember those to whom we owe so much in life, but also because all other virtues can be stated in terms of it and be developed from it. A familiar Chinese proverb has it that the best place to look for a loyal and good minister is in a family renowned for its filial piety.

Another point which should be made clear is the fact that, while Confucianism did emphasize the family as the basic social unit, it did not consider it to be the supreme object for loyalty in life. Loyalty to the family is the first in the order of sequence, but the interest of the family is definitely not the first in the scale of relative importance. The family is not an ultimate; it is only an intermediate, leading to larger social conceptions with their recognized higher claims. It is to be a stimulating incentive, and not a stumbling obstacle, in a man's larger social relations and greater social responsibilities. It was stated in the ancient records that when *Yu*, the Great, was a minister under Emperor *Shun*, and was engaged in the task of fighting the floods, he was so devoted to public service that he was continuously absent from his home for eight long years, during which time he thrice passed the very door of his house without going inside.[20] It was said that Confucius particularly praised him for such conduct.[21] This noble example set by great *Yu* has always been held up as the model and measure for devotion to public service and national welfare. Individuals in China may have failed to remember and live up to such ideals, but the teaching on the subject is quite clear.

Perhaps the most outstanding feature in the traditional Chinese family system is filial piety. Now what is filial piety? In the prominence given to ancestral worship by the early missionaries, through their vigorous condemnation of that practice as the most widespread idolatry in China, filial piety was looked upon as almost identical with ancestral worship. But it must be observed that the ceremony of "ancestral worship" has been only a part, and that not even the most important part, in the Confucian conception of filial piety. Respectful memory is indeed due one's parents, grandparents and great-grandparents, and other ancestors in a remote way; but respectful memory alone does not fulfill all that which is called for, nor, in fact, is it the greatest thing called for in filial piety. In general, we may say that filial piety requires that a person provide, liberally, respectfully, and affectionately, for

[20] Mencius, Bk. III. Pt. I. iv. 7.
[21] Mencius, Bk. IV. Pt. II. xxix. 1.

the needs and wants of the parents when they are alive and that he keep them in respectful memory when they have passed away. But, above all, it calls for noble living to maintain the honor and good name of the family. "Honor thy father and thy mother" is the essence or quintessence of the Confucian idea of filial piety. It has been fully recognized that the key word in this great commandment is the word "honor"; and honoring the family has been rightly taken to mean living worthily, nobly, and successfully. Confucius cited the ancient Emperor *Yao* as a superb example of great filial piety and explained his reasons for doing so by referring to the fact that *Yao* was, in virtue, a sage; in honor, an emperor; and, in wealth, having all within the four seas.[22]

Is ancestral worship really a form of worship? Much perhaps depends upon the psychology of the "worshiper." But three things may be pointed out in an attempt to answer the question. First, it is much more of a worship in Buddhism and Taoism than in Confucianism. Second, it was much more of a worship in the past than is the case at present, for the popular superstitious practices of burning paper money, lighting candles, spreading a feast before ancestral tablets or ances-

---

[22] The Great Learning xv. 1.

tral portraits have been largely done away with now. Where these practices are still continued they have become more and more symbolic ceremonies of respectful remembrance. Third, if it is "worship," it is quite different from any act of worshiping a god. The idea of seeking through such "worship" spiritual or supernatural blessing or protection has been either entirely absent or quite insignificant. Even in Buddhism and Taoism it is service by the living for the dead rather than help from the dead to the living.

The commandment, "Honor thy father and thy mother," as found in the Bible, carries with it a promise of reward, "that thy days may be long upon the land which the Lord thy God giveth thee." [23] It is interesting to note that the people who have paid the greatest attention to the observance of this commandment also happen to be the nation with the longest history. Shall we say that we see in this significant historical fact an example of the mysterious way God sometimes fulfills his purpose or carries out his promise? Filial piety has certainly contributed to the family solidarity in China. Has that in turn contributed to the social stability and historical continuity of the Chinese people and the Chinese nation?

[23] Exod. 20:12.

88

Whether or not we can find the rational explanation, we certainly have here a very interesting and significant coincidence.

5. *On Woman and Her Status.* Confucius said very little directly and specifically about woman in the "Four Books." Much more was found in the *Li Ki* (Record of Rites), which was a compendium of old teachings and principles collected by Confucius, rather than an exposition of his own thoughts and ideas. His principles are rules of universal application, without any distinction between man and woman. His only direct references are the recognition of the relationship between the husband and the wife as constituting one of the fundamental relations of life, and also two rather often-quoted statements for which he has been subjected to much criticism, although one of them was actually made by Mencius. These are (1) "that of the three acts of unfiliality the lack of heir or successor is the greatest";[24] and (2) "that it is hard to deal with women and little fellows (or immature persons), because intimacy breeds insubordination, and remoteness causes resentment."[25]   I doubt whether Confucius was talking about his wife when he was referring to women in general. In any case, I am sure Confucius would not make

[24] Mencius, Bk. IV. Pt. I. xxvi. 1.
[25] Analects xvii. 25.

89

such a statement today. If questioned on this point, he would, I believe, surely say: "I have grown much wiser since I made that careless statement some twenty-five centuries ago."

Confucius did not give woman as exalted a position as twentieth-century democratic and Christian standards would require, although it is very doubtful whether any religion at his time gave woman a better standing. Even Paul spoke of the husband as being the head of the wife, who should submit herself to him, and of the man as not created for the woman but the woman for the man.[26]

Confucius, or rather Confucianism, has been particularly blamed for having permitted, if not encouraged, concubinage through the importance attached to heirs. Strictly speaking, this condonement was not the explicit teaching of Confucianism but only a possible inference from it. The heir here referred to has generally been interpreted as a male issue from matrimony, but the word is really capable of a broader and newer interpretation. The exact word here used is *Hou*, meaning "after" or "successor." Lack of *Hou* or heir can therefore be expanded in its interpretation to mean the lack of somebody (or even something)

[26] Eph. 5:22-24; I Cor. 11:7-10.

to carry on not only a man's physical life and family name, but also his lifework, his cherished ideals, and his good influences. When *Yen Yuen*, the most favorite disciple of Confucius, died, the Master cried out, "Alas! Heaven has cut me off! Heaven has cut me off!" [27] This, I dare to believe, was the type of heir or successor Confucius cared for much more than a son to carry on his family name.

Surely Christians would agree with Confucianists that lamentable is the man concerning whom, when he dies, there can be nothing more said than "dust thou art, and unto dust shalt thou return." Pitiable indeed is the man who, when he dies, leaves nothing, or no one, behind him to trace his footprints on the sands of time and to push forward his noble mission in life and his worthy ideals. Modern Chinese are beginning to see that a man can live on in other ways than through the life of his son alone —for example, in bequeathing to educational, social, philanthropic, or religious institutions a part of the estate, which traditionally would go to lineal descendants.

Confucius could have done better, and concubinage could not be defended on any ground, even if restricted to the one condition of the lack of direct male issue. But in fairness to him it must

[27] Analects xi. 8.

be said that polygamy was a universal institution in the ancient world, existing in China long before the time of Confucius, and that the idea of permitting a secondary wife when there was no male offspring was in effect a great restriction rather than a liberal permission. I am glad to see concubinage outlawed in China by its modern law; but I am sorry that, at the same time, the wave of modern divorce is coming on in China also.

Actually, no man could have more than one wife under the old regime. In some respects the rule, "Those whom God hath joined together, let not man put asunder," held good in China even more strictly than in Western countries. For instance, in one way at least, the woman whom a man took to be his wife remained as his partner and equal both in life and in death. Even if the husband and wife should not agree with each other and not live much together in life, they would still be buried together after they died. Another woman might rob a wife of her husband's heart, but not her place and status as his "other half."

As a matter of fact, the woman in China has always occupied a very dignified and important place, though admittedly a less prominent and a somewhat subordinate and secluded position. The theory of *Yin* and *Yang* in the conception of the Cosmic Ultimate, and the placing of *Ch'ien* and

92

K'un, Heaven (father) and Earth (mother), as the first pair in the Eight Trigrams, showed that woman was considered the counterpart of man; no matter which half is considered the better half, she is certainly fully a half. The distinction between man and woman is not a horizontal division between the higher and lower half, but rather a vertical curving division[28] between the inner half (woman) ruling the home and the outer half (man) handling the outside affairs. Some such division of labor is not to be too vigorously condemned, for perhaps neither the home nor society can be what it should be unless there is some recognition of this principle of differentiation and coordination.

Accounts of outstanding women are not lacking in Chinese history. The powerful empress dowagers, the more than one "Joan of Arc," and the Chinese "George Eliot" of history are evidences showing that women in China cannot be conceived as having been altogether trampled under the heels of men. In the entire length of Chinese history there have been no other persons whose names are more honored and cherished by a grateful posterity and whose contributions are more

[28] Following the idea of the diagram of the *Tai Chi*, the Cosmos Ultimate:

appreciatively remembered than two noble women: the mother of Mencius, who changed her residence three times so that her son could be brought up in a proper environment, and the mother of *Yo Fei*, the famous general and great patriot who fought against the Tartars during the *Sung* Dynasty, and on whose back the mother had tattooed four characters, "Loyalty to the Utmost." The Chinese recognize that it was in both instances the mother who made the son, and that sometimes the hand that rocks the cradle can rule the world.

And, today, woman in no other country is so fully the equal of man in legal rights and social status as she is in China. No law of any country concerning inheritance or governing infidelity has more fully recognized the principle of the absolute equality of sexes than the modern Chinese law. This is perhaps the most radical change which has taken place in modern China; but the really amazing part of it is that both men and women have become so completely and so quickly adjusted to the new situation that they live as if it had been so from time immemorial. Perhaps the best illustration of this new situation is seen in the fact that in China today we have both a Generalissimo and a "Madamissimo," equally active in serving the nation, and almost equally popular with the people.

6. *On Politics and Government.* The Confu-

cian conception of the ideal state is often represented as a benevolent despotism; but in effect it is
a democratic monarchy—a monarchy in form, but
a democracy in spirit. The ideal state which Confucianism sought to set up, through the teachings
of Confucius, but more especially through those of
Mencius, is described in the classics as a government of the "kingly way," based upon benevolence
and righteousness. This was constantly and sharply
contrasted with a government of the "autocratic
way," built upon the strength of force. The basic
principle is still *Jen*, benevolent regard for others
—the ruler for his subjects, and the people for
each other.

The underlying political theory of Confucianism
is a curious mixture of the divine right of kingship
and the popular sovereignty of the people. The
king is the son of Heaven, and thus rules by
divine right. To Heaven he is supremely responsible—responsible as a dutiful son to obey and respect the wishes of Heaven, his Father. Thus far
he seems to have no responsibility to the people at
all. But the question arises, How is he to find out
the will of Heaven? When and how does Heaven
speak? The Confucian answer is: "Heaven sees as
the people see, and Heaven hears as the people
hear." [29] *Vox populi, vox Dei.* Therefore filial

[29] Mencius, Bk. V. Pt. I. v. 8.

95

piety to Heaven demands that the king "should like what the people like and should hate what the people hate." Mencius also declares: "In a nation the people are the most important, the state is next, and the ruler is the least important." [30] The king was to live for the people, and not the people for the king. *Noblesse oblige.* The totalitarian dictators surely would not have Confucius as a member of the Cabinet, nor Mencius as the minister of propaganda. For the people is not only above the king, but also above the state; the king is simply the agent, and the state the organization to serve the people.

If the king should disregard the welfare and interest of the people and go against their desires, then he would be flouting the will of Heaven as expressed through the people, and he would be guilty of unfilial conduct and therefore cease to be the exalted Son of Heaven, *Tien Tse.* Through this breach of trust he would lose his mandate, degrade himself to be "a mere fellow" to whom the people no longer owe allegiance, and whom it would be perfectly justifiable to depose. In fact, under such circumstances the man who headed a revolution was regarded as acting for Heaven in vindicating its righteous indignation. Such revolution was de-

[30] Mencius, Bk. VII. Pt. II. xv. 1.

scribed as "the falling of opportune rain" and "saving the people from water and fire." [31]

The political theory underlying the Chinese government has always been, even from time immemorial, a government for the people. Before the revolution of 1911, which set up the republic, the Chinese government was, in theory, a government of Heaven, through the king, for the people. Since the revolution, it has been a government "of the people, by the people, for the people." The spirit of the Chinese people has always been democratic, for even the old monarchy was built on essentially democratic principles.

In addition to this principle of the ultimate sovereignty of the people, there is another political theory upon which Confucianism insists—that a moral government, one which is built upon benevolence and righteousness, is not only the best government but also the strongest and the most permanent government.[32] A government which is most thoroughly in line with the interest of the people and in accord with their will is best able to mobilize the resources and strength of the nation. In Chinese political philosophy a state is therefore never just a power; it is a moral force.

7. *On the Golden Age of Grand Harmony (Ta*

[31] Mencius, Bk. III. Pt. II. v. 4-5.
[32] Mencius, Bk. II. Pt. I. v. 6.

Tung). What is the ideal state or community which Confucianism strives to build up? This is what Confucius had to say about it:

When the *Ta Tao* or Grand Way prevails (i.e., in the Golden Age), the world becomes a great commonwealth. Officers are selected because of their virtue; and appointments are made according to the abilities of the recipients. Mutual confidence is established and peaceful relations prevail. People regard not only their own parents as parents, nor only their own children as children. Provisions are made for the aged; employment is provided for the able-bodied; and guidance is given to the immature. Helpless widows and widowers, lonely orphans and childless people, and the crippled and deformed are all cared for. Men have their occupations and women have their homes. Useful articles are not to be thrown away, but they are not necessarily all kept as personal property. Labor is not to be idle, but work is not necessarily for the self only. Within such social atmosphere, selfish scheming and cunning intrigues are repressed, and banditry and rebellion do not arise. As a result there is no need of shutting the house gate at night. This is the state of real commonwealth and the Age of Grand Harmony (*Ta Tung*).[33]

This may not be an ideal state, perfect in every detail, but for all practical purposes it is perhaps a tolerably good enough community to live in. If it could be attained, Old Cathay would be veritably

[33] *Li Ki*, Bk. VII. i. 2.

a "Celestial" Empire. Utopian though it may be, it is the political and social goal which the Chinese people have had before them for at least twenty-five centuries.

It will be interesting to note, further, that the Chinese dream of a Golden Age is a state of Grand Harmony in a Great Commonwealth (*Ta Tung Shih Chieh*). It would be unnatural for the Chinese of old not to think of the "Middle Kingdom" as the center of the "new order," but I think it is historically accurate to say that it was conceived to be a center of cultural influence rather than one of physical force. Moreover, the Chinese mental vision has always gone beyond its own territorial limits—beyond the nation (*Kuo Chia*) to the world (*Tien Hsia*). That this vision of the whole world as a Commonwealth of Grand Harmony is not an old discarded idea, but still a living hope cherished in the hearts of the Chinese people, can be seen from the fact that the national song of China concludes its very first sentence with "*I Chien Min Kuo; I Chin Ta Tung*," that is, "to build the Republic and to promote Grand Harmony" (in the world).

VII. Reasons for the Enduring Influence of Confucius

As we thus review the influence of Confucius in the history and development of China, the question must arise in our minds, What has enabled Confucius to so rule the thought world of China and maintain, as it were, a kingdom of his own which is not of this world and which has outlasted all the dynasties of China? The answer is that he has accomplished this because he has been able to influence the Chinese people to accept and hold on to certain fundamental ideas, such as:

1. The thing of supreme importance is education. In China, the scholar, and not the millionaire or warrior, has always been looked upon as the one wearing the crown of life and waving the palm of success. In the traditional social scale the scholar always stands at the top.

2. Education involves both character building and knowledge or learning. Theoretically, a good scholar and a bad man are incompatible and impossible. The classical program of education, as expressed in the six pursuits of an educated man, consists of literature and mathematics to give him a foundation in liberal arts and science (intellectual development), rules of propriety to make him a cultured gentleman and the art of music to teach him the great value of harmony (moral training), and archery and charioteering to develop the body (physical training).

3. Education shall be for all men as well as for the whole man. Confucius said, "With education

100

there is no class distinction." [34] No one should be denied an education. Although even now universal education is far from being attained, a universal system of education had already been clearly outlined even before the time of Confucius; and while education and schools were not directly undertaken by the government until the beginning of the twentieth century, they had always been encouraged by the government.

4. Culture and moral character are the things which both make the man and make the nation. Speaking with reference to the individual, the Book of Great Learning[35] says, "With wealth, you can decorate the house; but with virtue, you adorn the personality." Looking at their nation, the Chinese always speak of the "Middle Kingdom" as "the land of pen and ink" [36] and "a nation of propriety and culture." It is also a country where the pen has always been considered as mightier than the sword.[37]

5. Spiritual values are far more precious than wealth and material things. Wealth and honor are

[34] Analects xv. 38.

[35] vi. 4.

[36] Literally, "land of essays and ink cakes," as the Chinese write with brush pens and make their own ink by rubbing a cake of ink on a stone inkstand.

[37] In a small book once almost universally used as a reader for beginners there is this passage: "Other persons may wear their sabers: I have a pen mightier than a sword."

but fleeting clouds; but virtue, achievement, and "words," that is, good character, public service, and wisdom and truth, are the three immortal things in life. These, therefore, are things for which we should strive.

Here we find some of the secrets of Confucius' great influence, greater than any king or empire builder. Is it not a very significant commentary on Chinese civilization and Chinese history that, whereas in our neighboring country in Asia the emperor is so high and "divine" that it would be sacrilegious for any person to speak of him in the same breath with any other man, however good and great he is, in China, no king, however great, would dare to consider himself the equal of Confucius?

VIII. Outstanding Accomplishments and Obvious Limitations[38]

Confucianism, at the root of Chinese culture, has produced one of the greatest and most enduring civilizations of the world. There is little doubt that it will not be found sufficient to answer all the problems of the modern age and meet all the requirements of human life, but neither is there any doubt that it has lasting qualities which are

[38] For further discussion see last chapter.

still valuable to China and perhaps to the world at large. We may at least say that a little more attention to the *technique of living*, which Confucianism so much emphasizes, will possibly give more balance and stability to the wonderful material and scientific achievements of the West in this great era of technical civilization.

The main text of the Book of the Doctrine of the Golden Mean concludes with a sublime vision of *Chung Ho*, the Perfect State of Equilibrium and Harmony. When this state of Grand Harmony is fully attained and universally achieved, it was therein said, "Heaven and earth will be in their place, and all things will be nourished and flourish." We may say that this Grand Harmony involves the harmonizing of three great laws of the universe: (1) the law of God (religion), (2) the law of man (morality), and (3) the law of matter (science), each fulfilling its own particular function. The West undoubtedly has excelled in the law of matter, and the East has undoubtedly emphasized the law of man; but both need to be adjusted and harmonized under the law of God. Then surely there will be Grand Harmony in the world.

In conclusion we may say that, while Confucianism has given to China a series of excellent lectures on the subject, "Thou shalt love thy neighbour as thyself," the Chinese will have to go to the Christian church for the great sermons on the yet more fundamental law of life, "Thou shalt love the Lord thy God with all thy heart, and with all thy soul, and with all thy mind, and with all thy strength."

It is certainly very interesting, and not altogether an unprofitable speculation, to imagine how Jesus Christ and Confucius would feel toward each other, and what they would say to or about each other, if they should meet in person. Would it be at all unnatural or unreasonable to suppose that Confucius would say with respect to Jesus Christ, "There cometh one mightier than I after me, the latchet of whose shoes I am not worthy to stoop down and unloose"? [39] And, on the other hand, could we imagine Jesus as saying, with reference to Confucius, something like this: "Behold an Israelite indeed, in whom is no guile!" [40] If this could be the spirit of the masters, what should be the spirit of their disciples?

[39] Mark 1:7.
[40] John 1:47.

104

III

BUDDHISM:
THE PATH OF ESCAPE

I. BUDDHISM IN CHINA

Place of Buddhism in China. Next to Confucianism, Buddhism has been perhaps the most influential factor in molding the thought and spiritual life of the Chinese people. In fact, if we put Confucianism outside of the category of religion, we may say that Buddhism comes nearer to being the religion of the Chinese than does any of its rival claimants. Its influence is felt in the religious views and in the philosophy of life, as well as in the literature, art, customs, and institutions of the Chinese.

Interesting Characteristics of Buddhism in China. Among the many interesting features and characteristics, the following may be particularly mentioned:

1. Buddhism has thrived in China, while it has practically died out in India. According to the generally accepted account, Buddhism was intro-

duced into China during the reign of *Ming Ti* of the Eastern Han Dynasty, that is, in the first century of the Christian era. Since then it has steadily broadened and deepened its grip upon the Chinese, while in India, the land of its nativity, it has gradually died out. It has disappeared in the land of its birth, but has become reincarnated and has thrived in the land of its "transmigration."

Two factors perhaps account for this unusual phenomenon. In the first place, Buddhism has found in China a much better climate and a more fertile soil for its growth than in Mother India. In its teaching of free salvation for all believers, Buddhism is irreconcilably opposed to the caste system of Hinduism; but it is quite in line with the fundamentally democratic spirit of the Chinese. In India the caste system, like the scorching sun, has made the earth too dry and hard for Buddhism to flourish. In China it has found a soil soft and moist, wherein the tender Bodhi Tree of Enlightened Wisdom can more easily strike root and grow strong.

In the second place, Confucianism, by confining itself to the practical problems of this life, has left the vast field of man's relation to God quite untouched. Confucianism has provided excellent food for the nurture of the humanistic side of the life of the Chinese, but has not supplied even a milk bottle for the distinctly religious side of man's life. Man, of all times and all climes alike, does not have his total needs and longings met by a purely humanistic philosophy or system of life, for, indeed, he does not, and cannot, live by bread alone. Into this vast and unoccupied field, therefore, Confucianism leaves the door wide open for Buddhism to enter.

2. Although Buddhism in China is in fact, and is known by all to be, a religion of foreign origin, it has become thoroughly indigenous. It is still fully Buddhistic, but it is also thoroughly Chinese. Buddhism is like a naturalized foreigner in China, who of course retains his foreign blood, but who has practically got rid of all his foreign manners. It is like one who is dressed in Chinese clothing, who speaks the Chinese language, and who even walks with a regular Chinese swing, and is thus able to live and mingle with the natives as a native. To use another figure, we may say that, although Buddhism did come from India, it is now no longer a pot plant transported from a foreign country; but it is a tree which has grown up on native soil. It is a Bodhi Tree grown from Bodhi seed, true to the species; but it differs from the original in that it has become an improved stock, due to better climate and more fertile soil, and perhaps also to a little different treatment.

3. Buddhism in China has a very interesting method of propagation. Up until the organization of modern Buddhist associations in recent years, Buddhism, unlike the Christian church, had made practically no effort to extend its faith through public preaching services. However, we may also say that preaching has been going on all the time, effectively though silently, and constantly though informally. This is done in three ways. First, it is done by dotting the whole country with temples situated at places of charming scenery and natural beauty. Tourists and people who go out on a holiday excursion will more likely than not find themselves heading toward a monastery, with a series of stone steps leading to it, perched or nestled at a prominent spot where the weary traveler can find a good resting place and where he may refresh his spirit by a cup of hot tea. The circumstances and environment are such that the more thoughtful, or anybody in a more thoughtful mood, will find in that experience a good Buddhist sermon—namely, that life itself is a pilgrimage, often involving a strenuous, difficult climb, and that in the Buddhist temple those who are weary and tired may find tranquillity and rest. Come hither, all ye who are weary and heavy laden! Secondly, much preaching is certainly done through silent messages, in well-selected mot-

toes and beautifully composed short statements, in couplet form, written on huge horizontal tablets and long hanging scrolls.[1] These are often very illuminating and inspiring—splendid thoughts expressed in exquisite phraseology, composed by prominent men and eminent scholars, and written in beautiful calligraphy which the Chinese so much admire. In this way they convey religious sentiments and ideas which will live long in the memory and thought of the reader. Thirdly, Buddhism exerts a powerful influence through its contribution to the literature, the art, and the customs of the nation. This includes both literature on Buddhism and Buddhist ideas in Chinese literature.

How Deeply Rooted Is Buddhism in China? Buddhism is now so deeply rooted in China that even if it were possible, by one sudden stroke, to

---

[1] They are something on the same order as our beautifully illustrated "Scripture motto cards"; but these horizontal tablets are often two to three feet wide and ten to twelve feet long, and these scrolls may be easily twelve or fifteen feet, or even more, in length.

I have recently come across some "Sentence Sermons" by the Rev. Roy L. Smith which furnish an even better analogy, such as:

"CONSIDER WELL—
The cost of a habit before you contract it.
The impotence of money before you give everything for it.
The short life of a lie before you tell one.
The value of a friend before you sacrifice one."

drive out all the monks and to destroy all the Buddhist temples, nevertheless it would continue to exist as a significant factor in the Chinese philosophy of life. Buddhism has succeeded in rooting itself in the life of the nation, not by trying to destroy the customs and traditions of the land, but very often by cleverly taking over and recasting them in the Buddhist mold. Thus, for instance, filial piety and ancestral worship were not a part of the "first century" Buddhism. But the early Buddhists did not fight against, and did not try to eliminate, these practices; they adopted them into their own system, by giving them a distinct Buddhist meaning and significance. China is said to be a land wherein the gentleman will not fight and the wise will not argue; if one person disagrees with another and does not believe in him, he will look at him but will leave him alone, with cold indifference. Buddhism wins its way to the very heart of the nation by saying to such people, as it were, "If you are too proud to fight, I will not hesitate to stoop to conquer."

What Are the Essential Teachings of Buddhism? The question is not an easy one to answer for several reasons. In the first place, Buddhism has not remained the same at all times and in all countries. In the second place, it has a very voluminous literature. What it has in the way of sacred books is not "a holy bible" of Buddhism but a whole library of "holy bibles." [2] In the third place, Buddhism also has its schools and "denominations." Both Hinayana Buddhism and Mahayana Buddhism are found in China—a juxtaposition which is suggestive of, if not comparable to, the Catholic and Protestant churches in Christendom. Of the ten Buddhist sects in China two belong to the Hinayana School and eight to the Mahayana School; and of the latter the two most important are the Ch'an (Zen) School or Meditative School and the Pure Land School, which believes in salvation by faith. But there are certain fundamental tenets held in common by all. An attempt will be made in the following paragraphs to set forth what we may call the general religious philosophy of Chinese Buddhism.

II. BUDDHISM AS A RELIGIOUS PHILOSOPHY

The Central Theme of Buddhism. The central theme and subject matter of Buddhism is the problem of suffering. That is the theme which gives it vitality and popularity. Buddhism ever lives in the life of mankind, and catches the ears of man, in spite of all its imperfections and inconsistencies, because in picking up the problem of suffering it

[2] The latest collection of Sutras printed in China was issued by the Shanghai Commercial Press, Ltd., in 1922. It had 7,148 sections in 1,757 books.

has put its finger on the most sensitive spot in man as he faces the problem of existence and ponders over the meaning of life. Suffering is a universal problem and an eternal concern of man. So, when Buddha says to the world, "Life is suffering," man responds, "So indeed have I found it." When Buddha says, "Follow me; I have found the way of escape," man says, "If it is so, I surely will go with you." There, I think, is the secret of the strength and appeal of Buddhism to mankind.

Life Pictured as a Sea of Suffering. What is the picture of life which Buddhism has painted for man? Perhaps the most general one is the picture of humanity being tossed, helpless and hopeless, on the angry billows of the stormy sea of suffering.[3] On this life's tempestuous sea, men are, each and all, struggling to get over to the "other shore," where they hope to find the land of blessed peace and tranquillity. But the story is always the story of failure to reach the desired haven; the feeble, ignorant human being has to go back to the same miserable world, through rebirth and transmigration, to start all over again, making the same trial, meeting the same failure, as it were, going through a process of repeating decimal ad infinitum.

---

[3] The Buddhists know how to make good use of visual education by representing this "sea" and other pictures of life and future life in their temples.

Thus, tens of thousands of Buddhists in China recite or chant, as many times a day as they have time to do it, the prayer or formula at the end of the Essence of Wisdom Sutra:

Ge-ta, Ge-ta, Pa-ra-ga-te
Pa-ra-sam-ga-te
Bodhi, Sva-ha,

which may be translated into English as follows:

Ferry, ferry, ferry over to the Other Shore!
Ferry all beings to the Other Shore!
Perfect Wisdom!   Hail! [4]

But to the vast majority of Chinese who chant this incantation in its original Sanskrit, its meaning is just as obscure as is the way it claims to show.

The Wheel of Karma.   While the parable of the ferry across the "sea of suffering" has a classical basis in Buddhist literature, a truer and more philosophical picture of the way of life, according to Buddhism, is the Wheel of Life which rotates unceasingly in accordance with the Law of Karma. This is the law of retribution—of effect following cause, of reward and punishment following deeds, of reaping following sowing, of man getting better and happier or lower and more miserable, in a continuous process of evolution and devolution.

[4] According to Prof. Shao-Chang Lee of the University of Hawaii, in his *Popular Buddhism in China.*

BUDDHIST CONCEPTION OF THE
WHEEL OF EXISTENCE[5]

[5] The Wheel of Existence is perhaps to be regarded more as an analysis of the basic factors or forces of the Buddhist conception of the eternal life cycle than an outline or summary of its philosophy of life.

The twelve *Nidanas* or links in the Causal Chain are not necessarily a chain of links in the sense that each of them is the antecedent cause of the next following; but they are the twelve "causes"—factors and forces—which link the "inner man" with the "outside world," and set in motion the wheel of life. Perhaps the best illustration is to say that the twelve

114

Nidanas form a sort of switchboard with switches which can turn on the current of life and set the Wheel of Karma to turn.

The twelve *Nidanas* are often symbolically represented or pictorially presented as follows:

1. Ignorance or lack of enlightenment by a blind woman led by a man.
2. Motion or activities by a potter making earthenware.
3. Consciousness or cognition by a restless monkey.
4. "Names" and "Colors," i.e., tangible and intangible objects, by a boat rocking in the waves.
5. The "Six Entrances" or the six "roots of life"—i.e., the five physical senses, eyes, ears, nose, tongue and body, and the psychic sense, the mind—by a building under construction.
6. Contact or "touch" by a man and a woman sitting together and embracing each other.
7. Impressions or "receiving" by a man with an eye pierced by an arrow.
8. Cravings or "love" by a man trying to quench his thirst by drinking intoxicating wine.
9. Grasping or "taking" by a man filling a basket with fruits picked from a tree.
10. Possession or "having" by a pregnant woman.
11. Birth by a woman in childbirth.
12. Old Age and Death by an old man overladen with a heavy burden and about to die.

(The above English terms for the twelve *Nidanas* are direct translations from Chinese Buddhist literature. Dr. Paul Carus, in his book *The Dharma*, gives them as follows: (1) ignorance, (2) organized formation, (3) sentiency, (4) name and form, (5) the six fields, (6) contact, (7) sensation, (8) thirst, (9) craving, (10) growth, (11) birth, and (12) old age, death, sorrow, etc. Dr. J. B. Pratt, in his book *The Pilgrimage of Buddhism*, page 75, uses the following terms: (1) ignorance, (2) disposition, (3) cognition, (4) name and form, (5) five senses and the mind, (6) contact, (7) feeling, (8) craving, (9) grasping or attachment, (10) becoming, (11) birth, and (12) old age, sickness, death.)

Life, or the Life Process, is represented by a Wheel of Life, which in Buddhist mythology is held in the hands of the Evil One, Mara, the Devil. There are three sections to this wheel. (1) The hub, or innermost section, presents a picture of the "three root-evils" [6] inherent in man's heart: ignorance or insanity, desire or cravings, and hatred. These three are represented pictorially by a pig, a bird (which may be a dove, an eagle, or a cock), and a serpent. (2) The six sections within the spokes indicate the six worlds or phases of life, in the process of reincarnation and transmigration, namely, heaven, man, demons, beasts, hungry ghosts, and hell. (3) On the outer rim are represented the twelve links in the chain of *Nidanas*, or the concatenation of cause and effect.

According to this picture of the Wheel of Life, it is the inherent badness in the human heart, when stimulated into action by the twelve *Nidanas*, that causes the Wheel to turn, producing deeds which must be adjusted according to the law of Karma.

To this Wheel of Karma all sentient beings are forever chained. Through sin and misdeed man is eternally indebted to Karma (retribution), from

[6] These three root-evils are also spoken of as "the three poisons of life." They are the sources of all the disturbances and annoyances of life.

116

debt

which no release can be had until the last farthing
is paid; however, the balance of account in each
life, from merits and demerits, is likely to be against
rather than for him. Therefore, as a slave of sin,
man is forever chained to the Wheel as a debtor
of Karma.

From this chain of cause and effect which binds
the man to this dark, miserable world, the only way
of salvation is the way of escape. Buddhism is not
bold enough nor optimistic enough to hope for
victory and triumph. It would be quite satisfied
if only emancipation and release could be secured.

Now what is the way of escape? As ignorance
is the root of all evil, so wisdom and enlightenment
are the only remedy and solution. If we suffer
because of the curse of our own deceptive illusions,
then we shall cease to suffer when this veil of inner
darkness is lifted; and we shall dwell in the light
of illuminating wisdom. This was the great discovery made of Buddha when, after sitting under
the Bodhi Tree for forty-nine days in deep meditation and intense earnestness, he had his great Awakening and found the Perfect Wisdom which
illuminated his whole soul.

Now what was this "heavenly vision" which
brought him from darkness into the marvelous light,
and which gave him release from the bondage of
suffering and the confidence that he could thereby

117

and thereafter be the bearer of the torch of True Light? It was a perfect vision of the true nature of life, or a complete answer to the fundamental and penetrating questions of human existence: Who are we? What are we? What is in us and what are we in? In other words, it was a thorough exposition of the problem of life leading to the discovery of a satisfactory solution.

This "revelation" was summed up in the Four Noble Truths. They are the great certainties and basic facts of life and are as follows:

1. That life is suffering.
2. That desire is the cause of suffering.
3. That by bringing about the cessation of desire we can put an end to the cause of suffering, and thus remove suffering itself.
4. That the way for the elimination of desire is through adhering to the Eightfold Right Path.

Buddhist philosophy starts with the basic assumption that all life involves suffering—physical pain, mental anguish, disappointed hopes, frustrated desires, etc., etc. Life is but a lamentable journey from birth to death. Time pushes man on to old age; death holds him in its stern relentless hand; and suffering in one form or another disturbs his peace and mars his happiness. Life is a drama with four scenes: birth, old age, sickness, and death. Even inanimate objects cannot escape this law of

118

change and decay, for mountains may crumble down and streams may dry up.

What is suffering? In the last analysis, suffering is disappointed hopes, unrealized desires, and unsatisfied cravings. If such be the case, it is apparent that the root of all evil and the cause of all suffering is to be found not so much in external circumstances as inside our own selves—in our inner desires, cravings, thirst, appetite, covetousness, and lust. We are annoyed, disturbed, distressed, and disappointed because that which we desire to have, we have not; that which we desire to avoid, we must endure. Life is full of suffering, because we are full of desires. So long as desires exist, there will always exist pain and suffering or the possibility of pain and suffering.

Now what can we do in this terribly bad situation? Evidently there are only two ways of dealing with this problem of suffering and frustrated desires: either bring about the satisfaction of all our desires, or work for their entire elimination. Since the first alternative is impossible and inconceivable, the second is the only one possible. Therefore, the only sure and proper way of eliminating all suffering is to eliminate all desires. No one could feel disappointed, disturbed, and distressed in not having what he desired not. Blessed,

119

therefore, is he who has no desire for anything; for he will never be disappointed.

But by what ways and means can we reach this goal, and attain this objective? The answer is, through the unswerving adherence to the Eightfold Right Path. To be on this right path we must keep ourselves, rigidly and constantly, in the right —right in thought and deed, in mood and frame of mind, in understanding and perspective. In other words, we should strive to be always right: in seeing, in thinking, in speaking, in doing, in living, in effort, in idea, and in attitude.

But, again, what is right seeing and right thinking, so that we may have the right attitude toward life and may exert our effort in the right direction? The answer is that this "right seeing," which starts us out on this Eightfold Path, is the understanding and insight to see through the miserable deceptive transiency of the world. And this, in Buddhism, means to have the wisdom to know that there is nothing real in the world. What is in the world is certainly no more, and may be less, than the motes which people a ray of sunshine in the shade. Buddhism therefore calls man to wake from the great delusion and realize that the alluring material objectives of life are but "colored dust." [7]

[7] More literally, "red dust," red being the color so gorgeous and attractive.

Therefore, in the final analysis, the great Enlightenment in Buddhism is the light which will enable us to see that, in truth and reality, all things, including even our own very being, are empty and nonexistent. They are only echoes in an empty valley, or images in a glass mirror. All that we see in the world is but evanescent form and color, behind which there is no real existence or substance. The unenlightened ones are all first-class *ignoramuses*, who delude and deceive themselves in taking what is unreal as real, and what is nonexistent as existent. The enlightened persons see through these semblances, and understand that that which the ignorant takes as real or existing is really unreal and nonexisting.

In other words, to the Buddhist the world is purely subjective. To him there is no objective reality in the outside world. Life is but a dream; the world is but a make-believe phenomenon. Whatever there is, is not. That which we desire to have, crave to possess, and lust to grasp—all are deceptive illusions, the creatures of our imagination, born of the vanity and badness of the human heart. Thus it is taught in the Essence of Wisdom Sutra:

> Matter (color and form) is not different
>   from emptiness;

121

> Emptiness is not different from matter;
> Matter is emptiness;
> Emptiness is matter.

We cannot see anything in Buddhism until we can understand and appreciate this conception of "nothingness" in Buddhism.

The whole world of apparent being is the product of interaction of cause (*Yin*) and its accessory condition (*Yuen*), or of the primary cause and the secondary cause.[8] The cause is the origin and root of "being"; the accessory condition (secondary cause) is the circumstance or the factor which brings the cause into being. This secondary cause is a sort of intermediary between the originating cause and the produced effect. For instance, the seed of a plant is the cause, its planting in the ground and cultivation by a farmer is the accessory

[8] This relationship is expressed in Chinese by the correlatives *Yin* and *Yuen*, cause and relations, which is a relationship quite different from that expressed in the correlatives, *Yin* and *Kou*, cause and effect. We are all accustomed to the idea of the cause producing the effect, which is the ordinary theory of *Yin-Kou*; but Buddhism has gone a step further by analyzing the concept of *Yin* or cause into two component parts: the basic material fact, which goes under the name *Yin*, and the relative or concurrent active force, which sets the basic fact in operation to produce the effect (*Kou*). This second factor in the *Yin*, or cause, is known as *Yuen*, the secondary but the dynamic force in the chain of causation. If *Yin-Kou* can be explained in the diagram, cause→effect, *Yin-Yuen* can be illustrated by the equation, $Yin + Yuen = $ effect.

condition, and the resulting plant (the bringing of the plant into being) is the effect.

There are two constituent elements in all "being": namely, the apparent object in the outside world, and the mental or psychological faculties inside the man. Nothing comes into being unless and until the external stimulus and the internal response co-exist, and there is a meeting within the mind. Thus, a visible object comes into being only when the faculty to see meets the object to be seen. So, to a blind man, or to one who has eyes but sees not, there is nothing visible, because there is not present the faculty to see, though the object to be seen is present. In the same way, to a person who is deaf, or who has ears but hears not, there is nothing audible. To such a person who is blind or who chooses to be blind, there exists no object of beauty which has any attraction, nor scene of horror which can produce fear.

From this fundamental postulate it follows that there is only so much of a world and such kind of a world as is created by our own mind and desire. If such be the case, then by regulating our desire we can regulate the kind of world we live in; and, *a fortiori*, by suppressing or eliminating all desires we can eliminate the world altogether. When a man's desire ceases to stir, then the world ceases to exist for him; and he is, as the Christians would say, "dead to the world." When the "cause" stops, then the "effect" ceases to be produced; and the law of cause and effect (Karma) ceases to operate. All depends upon whether one has the understanding to see through the process. To the truly enlightened, this is perhaps as plain as daylight and as simple as A.B.C.! But, to be thus enlightened— what an achievement!

Now if such is the world we are living in, what about life itself? The answer is that life also is empty. "I" do not exist. "I am" is simply an illusion of an individual's thought. Life in its static form is but a bundle of sensations and desires; in its dynamic form it is just a stream of ever-changing and nonabiding consciousness, which passes out of existence as soon as it comes into being. It dies as soon as it is born. Everything is transient and impermanent. Therefore, to a person who has attained Perfect Enlightenment, "there is no form, no sensation, no idea, no will, no consciousness. . . . . There is neither world of vision nor world of thought and consciousness." [9] Thus, in its extreme view, Buddhism denies even the existence of the *ego*, the personality or the soul of man. Both Christianity and Buddhism teach that man should enter the narrow gate; but if Christianity demands

[9] Essence of Wisdom Sutra.

that a rich man cannot enter into the Kingdom of Heaven without leaving his possessions outside, Buddhism demands that he must leave even himself outside. We are in the world, but not of the world. The correct way of living is therefore the way of the absent-minded professor who, though physically present in the world, nevertheless lives, in thought and consciousness, only in the realm of his special interest. The world of immediate consciousness is the only world we really live in. Life is indeed just a passing show.

Life is, therefore, like a geometrical point; it indicates a position, but has no dimensions—neither length, nor breadth, nor thickness. No such point ever exists in our common everyday experience. But it does exist in theory. In fact, it is fundamental to the whole science of geometry. Again, it may be said that life is like the flickering flame of a burning candle. It is always the same; but it is also never the same. It exists, but does not remain in existence. It manifests itself through consuming itself.

Yet, although life is elusive and empty, it has, at the same time, immense and immeasurable magnitude. According to Buddhism, all life belongs to one ubiquitous, even though really nonexistent, unity and entity. Our human life is linked up with the Buddha-life above and with the animal-life

125

below. Every man has in himself a potential Buddha, which makes it possible for him to attain Buddhahood.[10] He has also in himself the beast, to which he may degenerate. This is the life process, according to the law of Karma, through transmigration and reincarnation.

The modern evolutionists really have not discovered anything very new. For, as to developing a theory of evolution, Gautama Buddha antedated them by more than twenty centuries. And he did a more thoroughgoing job, for his theory of evolution is not a one-way street but a two-way avenue; it works both ways, curving upward as well as curving downward. Not only can the Buddhist exhibit his wisdom by claiming to have come up from a monkey; on the other hand, he can, if he likes, go back to be a monkey, or even a donkey, if he so prefers. In fact, he will be one, if he is not careful.

Furthermore, life has not only infinite breadth; it has unlimited length and duration. To anybody who says that he would like to live his life over again, Buddha says, "Indeed, you shall! There is

[10] The "Lotus Sutra" (*Fa-hua Ching*) refers to this as the "Buddha-seed"; and the "Nirvana Sutra" (*Nieh-Pan Ching*) refers to it as the "Buddha-nature." Reichelt has an interesting discussion and an attractive pictorial presentation of this idea in his book *Truth and Tradition in Chinese Buddhism*, pages 327-30.

no way out of it!" Each of us is not living in one
world, but in three different worlds—past, present,
and future. We came, at the time of our birth,
from the world-past to the world-present, and we
pass on, at the time of our death, from the world-
present to the world-future. We are, as it were,
all traveling salesmen, always "on the go." We
are all children of eternity, forever going round
and round in a merry-go-round, changing from
one seat to another at each grand stop—sometimes
sitting in a limousine, sometimes riding on a bicy-
cle, while at other times we may be mimicking and
prancing like a horse.

In this life process from eternity to eternity, the
rule of the game is that we must always start from
where we left off before. We are what we are,
because of what we were before; and we will be
what we will be, because of what we are now. Not
only do we sow the seed from which we will have
to reap, but we inherit from our previous life the
"root" for good and evil from which springs the
tree of this life, which in turn bears fruit from
which will spring the new "root" for our next
existence.

Such being the contents and consequences of this
life—so frail our human nature, so overwhelming
the forces of evil, and so unrelenting the law of
Karma—the only thing for man to do is to run

away as quickly as possible from the "city of destruction" in which we are doomed, like Christian in Bunyan's *Pilgrim's Progress*.

But where to? Buddha says, to Nirvana, the land of eternal rest and bliss. But again we would ask, What is Nirvana? and Where is Nirvana? Like all conceptions of the Ultimate or Absolute, the term is difficult to explain and define. But in general it may be described as a state of perfect peace and tranquillity. According to Hinayana Buddhism it is the "extinction of illusion"; according to Mahayana Buddhism it is the "attainment of truth." The two views are not so radically different, being the positive and negative sides of the same principle. According to the positive and more preferable explanation, Nirvana means the state of mind in which desire (*upadana*), error (*klisa*), and thirst (*tanha*) are extinct and the mind has attained a happy state of enlightenment, where there is peace of mind, bliss, the glory of rightness in this life and beyond, and finally the eternal rest of Buddha after death. In Chinese this idea is expressed in the term *Mih Tu*, which, being interpreted, means "extinction" (i.e., of self and its desires) and "crossing" (i.e., from suffering to bliss).

Where is Nirvana? The answer is that Nirvana, like the Kingdom of Heaven, is within the man.

It must begin there, although it does not end there. A person must have Nirvana within his heart in this life before he can enter Nirvana after death. There are two stages of Nirvana: a preliminary stage, which is an imperfect state that a man can have right now and here; and the perfect state, which the enlightened soul enters after death. The first is known as Nirvana, which is limited or relative, and the second as Pari-nirvana, or the Super-nirvana, which is unlimited and absolute.

This distinction corresponds to the three stages or states of enlightenment which a man may enter. Enlightenment is divided into the enlightened mind (first step), and the enlightened life, that is, a life devoted to the enlightenment of others (second step), and the perfect enlightenment (third step), which is attained when the fully enlightened mind completes its redeeming mission in a fully enlightened life. Hinayana stops with the first step and attains "limited Nirvana," whereas Mahayana pushes on through the fully enlightened life until it attains Pari-nirvana and veritable Buddhahood.

Correspondingly there are also three different degrees of attainment. First, we have the *Lohans* (Arahat or Arhat), those who have attained enlightenment and Buddhist salvation for themselves. Second, we have the *P'u-sas* (Bodhisattva), those

129

who have found enlightenment and release from the bondage of the world, but who choose to remain in it in order to enlighten and save others. Third, we have the Buddhas, those who have reached the ultimate achievement and entered Nirvana, the state of eternal bliss. Big Buddhist temples in China usually have a Hall of Five Hundred Lohans; but, of course, the chief object of worship and adoration in the temples is the *P'u-sa*, ever-compassionate and helpful to the worshipers.

This concept of Nirvana, the state of bliss, which represents the highest aspiration of Buddhism, is essentially negative in nature. It is a state in which there is no evil to cause suffering, no annoyance to disturb the soul; in it one can completely relax, being freed from all worry and care, and can say to oneself, "Now, rest thee, O my soul. I am at last at the end of life's troubles. Enjoy peace and tranquillity." It is no doubt a state of serene tranquillity, of peace which passes understanding; but there is no exultant joy and active happiness. There is no singing of songs of triumph, but only sighs of relief. The great awakening[11] frees man from life's evil dreams, but does

[11] The Chinese word for "to be awakened" is *Chio*, which means to feel or come back to your senses. A good illustration of this state of mind is seen in the story of the prodigal son "when he came to himself" and said, "I will arise and go to my father," etc.

130

not fill it with positive happiness. In fact, the way of salvation is so long and difficult that the objective, if and when finally achieved, would make one feel like an athlete who wins a marathon race—gratified in heart that he has finally succeeded, but too exhausted to enjoy anything except to relax and lose consciousness.

The idea is so remote and abstract, and the process involved is so long and difficult, that very few people have a heart stout enough even to hope for its achievement. We are told that even Buddha himself could attain Enlightenment only because of merits accumulated through ever so many transmigrations in previous existences. It is an idea which may inspire our hope, but it is a star so high in the height of heaven that if we should ever succeed in hitching our wagon to the star, the wagon itself would surely be dangling in the air. To the average Buddhist, of real and immediate concern is the hope and prospect of being reborn into a little higher state or a slightly better life in the next life.

The way of salvation as outlined by original Buddhism was more difficult and forbidding than climbing up an overhanging rock. So Hui-yuan, a Chinese monk who lived in 333-416, started the Pure Land School, and preached the doctrine of "salvation by grace through faith" in the Amitabha Fu (Buddha of Infinite Splendor), through whose

131

grace the believer may be born after death into Western Paradise, variously known in Buddhistic literature as "Pure Land," "Western Heaven," and "Land of Supreme Happiness." The way to get there is not merely by means of small good works, but by keeping in mind, with thoughts undisturbed, the Amitabha Buddha, constantly relying upon him and calling upon his name. Thus, no prayer is repeated so often by so many people in China as "*Nan-Mo O-Mi-T'o Fu*," which is to say, "Hail to thee, Amitabha Buddha," or "I turn to Amitabha Buddha, in reverence and trust." This prayer is not only on millions of lips in China; but it is found carved everywhere on stone pillars and written in big characters on the walls outside of the temples and in other public places.

The Land of Bliss to which Amitabha Buddha will take his believers is a much more attractive place. It is much more in line with the conception of paradise which is current in other religions. Indeed, there is so much similarity to the picture of paradise given in the Christian Bible that a question has been raised as to whether the Pure Land School had been influenced by the Nestorian missionaries, who started out in China at the same time and place as the Pure Land School. In the Buddhabhasata-Amitayah Sutra there is a description of the Buddhist paradise which runs as follows:

It is called the Land of Supreme Happiness, because all beings there do not suffer from any mental or physical pain, and only enjoy pleasures and happiness of all kinds. . . . . In this Land of Supreme Happiness there are seven lakes, all adorned with gems. These lakes are filled with water which possesses eight good qualities, namely, liquidity and purity, refreshing coolness, sweetness, softness, calmness, productive power of giving life to vegetation, and power of satisfying hunger and quenching thirst. The bottoms of these lakes are strewn with golden sand. . . . . Again, there are many wonderful birds of many colors . . . . singing in concord. Melodiously they proclaim the five virtues (faith, fortitude, ascertainment of truth, meditation, and wisdom), the five powers, which are acquired by the practice of these virtues, the seven Bodhi paths leading towards the attainment of Enlightenment, and the Eight Noble Paths leading to the highest state of bliss.

This sect, which is also known as the Lotus Sect, is the most popular and has the largest following in China.

III. BUDDHISM IN ACTION

In addition to the religious philosophy of the Buddhists, it may be interesting to note some of the virtues which are particularly cultivated by the followers of Buddha.

1. *Kindness and Compassion.* This is perhaps the first thing which we would notice in the atti-

133

tude and spirit of a devout Buddhist. Kindness (*Tzu*) is to impart happiness; and compassion (*P'ei*) is to remove suffering. They are of course akin to, and grow out of, love; but in comparison they are more quiet and subdued in their expression. However, what they lack in activity and assertiveness is perhaps made up in naturalness and spontaneity. To the truly devout Buddhist, kindness and compassion are not only the practice of a virtue but the expression of a transformed nature. This attribute of Buddha is best expressed in the *Kwan Yin* or the Goddess of Mercy, who is forever cruising on the "sea of suffering" on a Lotus Flower to find and rescue the lost and perishing. She is the most popular, as well as the most interesting, Bodhisattva (in Chinese just *P'u-sa*) in the Buddhist pantheon; for *Kwan Yin* was a man in Hindu Buddhism, but became a woman when he transmigrated and was reincarnated in China.

The scope of Buddhist kindness and compassion is not limited to human beings; it extends to include consideration for all animals, birds, fish, insects, and even to trees and plants, but particularly to everything which is of flesh and blood. This attitude is perfectly natural and logical when we bear in mind that the Buddhist conception of life is a cosmological one.

In line with this principle of kindness and compassion, the first commandment of Buddhism is not to kill, that is, not to take or destroy life in any form. From this, two very interesting and very widely prevalent customs have grown up. The first is vegetarianism, that is, to refrain from taking any meat or fish, and to eat only vegetables. This may be done either on certain days of the month, such as the first and fifteenth, or for a short period, or at all times, that is, in every day of the year. The second is the practice of paying for any captured animals or fish, and then restoring them to their freedom. In almost every big temple there is a "pool of redemption" where such redeemed fish are kept. Often we also find that certain waterways or some particular section of water is declared to be an "open city" where no fishing is permitted.

2. *Meekness and Nonviolence.* Every Buddhist, whether priest or layman, is exhorted to be meek and to practice nonviolence or nonresistance. When reviled, he reviles not, but is to control himself and to convert others by repeating *"Nan-Mo O-Mi-T'o Fu."* When struck by others, he is not supposed to strike back. It is perhaps reasonable to expect that, when too much exasperated, he may lose his Buddha temper for the moment and return the "courtesy." On the whole, however, a Buddhist is perhaps likely to take a more serious view

135

of the injunction, "Whosoever shall smite thee on the right cheek, turn to him the other also"; in any case, he will perhaps be less likely to hit back than most of us Christians, or at least to hit back so quickly or so hard. The conscientious objector will find many Buddhists who will share his views.

3. *Charity and Almsgiving.* Among the positive virtues emphasized by Buddhism, the first is charity and almsgiving. This is the first of the six ways of crossing (*paramita*) the ocean of birth and death, or the restlessness of worldly life (*samsara*), over to Nirvana. (The other five *paramita* are morality, patience, zeal, meditation, and wisdom.) In this respect, the Buddhists were the forerunners in China of the Salvation Army in attending to the needy and hungry.

What is particularly noteworthy in this connection is their teaching that the greatest charity, that form of almsgiving which will secure the greatest merit for the benefactor, is the diffusion of the knowledge of wisdom. In the eleventh and thirteenth sections of the Diamond Sutra it was emphatically pointed out that, although great blessing would be acquired by good men and good women if they would use all the seven treasures of the world, and would even sacrifice their lives for the sake of charity, even greater blessing would be obtained by accepting the Sutra, and explaining it to others. This is the teaching which imbued the Buddhists with fervent missionary zeal, and which made it the first religion in the world actually to become international.

4. *Reflection and Meditation.* Buddhists not only understand that it takes time to be holy, but they are actually willing to spend the time for it. All devout Buddhists are well versed in the art of meditation and reflection. The simple-minded merely learn to repeat some simple Buddhist formula or prayer over and over again, counting it off on a string of beads—for example, a rosary of sandalwood or dry lotus seeds, which the person holds in his hand while so used, and which he wears as a necklace when not in use. Often they do not understand the meaning of the prayer they are repeating; but, just the same, it helps to put them in a deeply meditative, quiet, and prayerful mood. The more learned often have a definite period set apart each day for "sitting in meditation," when they are to empty their thoughts, particularly any thought which forms an attachment to material possessions and physical pleasure. This is their daily spiritual exercise to lift them from the annoyance and disturbance of the noisy world below, up through the foggy clouds by which the world is enveloped, to the top of the "mount of transfiguration." This is the Buddhists' "morning

watch," to keep their hearts pure, so that they can see the truth and learn to dwell in the truth.

5. *The Lotus and the Pure Heart.* The Lotus Flower is almost inseparably linked with Buddhism as its most popular religious symbol. Except when represented as riding on some particular favorite animal, the classical and traditional form of the statue of Buddha is one standing or sitting on a pedestal carved in the shape of a lotus flower. The lotus is significant as a flower which rises out of the water, but which remains above and untouched by the water. What a splendid objective sermon on the meaning and ideals of Buddhism! Just imagine yourself looking at a lotus, a big flower of white color or quiet pink, beautiful and fragrant, grown from a root immersed in the slimy, dirty mud under the water, but rising high above its surface, pure, lovely, unsoiled. Imagine again looking at such a flower in the fresh air of early morn; on its big leaves, spreading themselves out as inverted umbrellas, there stand a few drops of morning dew, like pure crystals on the rich, green velvet of the supporting leaves. How dainty and lovely, pure and quiet, as life should be! Think again how serene and steady the dewdrop remains when it is allowed to remain quiet and undisturbed, but how easily it rolls off and disappears if allowed to be disturbed. In this little

parable of nature a sympathetic observer can see the whole story of the meaning and teaching of Buddhism: how exquisitely beautiful is the lofty nobleness of Buddha life, how serene and quiet this meditative spirit, how immaculately pure this enlightened life-purpose—how free from the low and base, and from the selfish and ignoble! In the Lotus Flower, its most popular symbol, we see the intrinsic nobleness and beauty in the Buddhist ideal of life, the meaning and lesson Buddha tries to teach unto mankind.

IV

TAOISM:
THE LAW OF NATURE

I. LAO-TZE AND TAOISM

China as a Land of Three Spiritual Kingdoms.
The most romantic period of Chinese history is
the period of the Three Kingdoms. It furnished
the material for China's Sir Walter Scott to produce the greatest and most popular historical novel
in all its literature, *The Story of the Three Kingdoms.* One of the best-known episodes in that
novel, which is often enacted upon the stage, is
"The Three Sworn Brothers of the Peach Gar-
den" who established the Kingdom of Shu in West
China. It is in that region of "Free China" where
the great movement "China Rediscovers Her West"
—brilliantly portrayed in the symposium of that title
by Yi-Fang Wu and Frank W. Price—is now so
significantly going on.

In the world of religion we may say that there
is a parallel situation. Confucianism, Buddhism,
and Taoism may be regarded as the three spiritual
kingdoms of China. While they were not so par-

140

ticularly affectionate to each other as to lead us to speak of them as three sworn brothers, nevertheless Confucius, Sakyamuni (Buddha), and Lao-tze did form a great triumvirate of the religious leaders of China. Of this trio, Lao-tze was decidedly the junior partner in influence, although he was the most elderly in appearance and in statuary and pictorial presentation, actually the senior in date of birth, and exceeded the other two in longevity of life.

Lao-tze, meaning the Old Philosopher, but sometimes spoken of as the "Great Old Boy" and sometimes as the "Grand Old Master," was perhaps China's deepest thinker and greatest mystic. A senior contemporary of Confucius, he lived in the same age as Buddha in India, and Jeremiah and Ezekiel among the prophets of Israel. His whole life and personality had a halo of mysticism over it. According to Sze-Ma Chien, the Herodotus of China—in the picturesque translation of Paul Carus —he was born "in the hamlet of Good Man's Bend, Grind Country, Thistle District, Bramble Land"; or, to be a little more simple and lucid, in the present province of Honan, Central China. Legend has it that even at his birth he had white hair and the countenance of an old man, and that he announced his own name as soon as he came to earth.

141

We know very little of his life except that he was custodian of the archives of the Dynasty of Chow. Sze-Ma Chien described him as a man who "practiced reason and virtue and that his doctrine aimed at self-concealment and namelessness." He denounced the turmoil of the age, and prophesied the decay of the existing state. Evidently in despair and disgust, at the venerable age of over eighty, he finally left the country, wandered to the unknown West, and thus became mysteriously lost to the world.

At the request, or rather upon the insistence, of the border officer, he wrote, before he finally crossed the boundary, the Tao-Teh-King or the Canon of Reason and Virtue (literally, "Truth and Virtue Classic"). This is a book of about five thousand words divided into eighty-one short chapters, in which he set forth his philosophy of life. It was possibly the best-treasured "oriental puzzle," fascinating and much admired, but perhaps not much understood by anybody.

His life and influence perhaps can be best summed up as follows: In China's distant past there once lived a great thinker, who caught a grand vision of a new way of life. This vision is his sublime conception of the *Tao*, The Way, or The Truth, of which the only original sketch-picture we have is his Tao-Teh-King. We may perhaps best describe it, using the language of an artist, as an antique picture done in modernistic style. To most unlearned amateurs, it appears to be just a conglomeration of fantastic pictures executed in brilliant colors; but there are many experts who look upon it as a great masterpiece.

Lao-tze was the founder of the Taoist school of philosophy, and has been taken by Taoism as the founder of the religion bearing that name. But the Taoist philosophy and the Taoist religion are very different from each other. By way of comparison, two Smiths or two Browns may have the same family name, but they may not look at all like each other; they may even be such distant cousins that they can hardly be regarded as real relatives. This was the case with the Taoist philosophy and the Taoist religion. Though the historical relationship or connection between the two can be clearly seen and easily traced, they hardly resemble each other.

Taoism as a religion did not grow directly out of the philosophy of *Tao* as expounded by Lao-tze in his Tao-Teh-King, although, through later developments, both Lao-tze and the Tao-Teh-King have now become integral parts of Taoism. Lao-tze lived and taught in the sixth century B.C., while Taoism as a religion was not organized until the second century A.D. by Chang Tao-Ling. (Some

143

have thought that his original name was simply
Chang Ling and that the middle character in his
name, the word "tao," was a later addition.)   In
its beginning, this religious sect was really a sort of
secret society with a political motive.   The true
relationship between the Taoist religion and the
Taoist philosophy was said to be that Taoism needed a sacred book, but had none; so it borrowed the
Tao-Teh-King for the purpose.   Neither had it an
outstanding figure as a founder; so it adopted Lao-
tze as the "Father" of that religious system.   Being
a secret society, the mysticism of Lao-tze and his
philosophy, by this very fact, could serve a useful
purpose for the new organization.

II. Taoism as a Philosophy

The Doctrine of Tao.   In the philosophy of
Lao-tze, the doctrine of *Tao*—The Truth or The
Way—as found in the Tao-Teh-King, is the cornerstone of the whole system.   But what is *Tao* is difficult to explain and define.   Lao-tze himself made
confusion worse confounded by saying in the very
opening sentence of the Tao-Teh-King that "the
Tao which can be expressed or defined is not the
constant or invariable *Tao;* and the name which can
be named is not the constant or invariable name."
He therefore makes no secret of the fact that in

144

inviting you to join him in an expedition of exploration in his field of philosophical speculation he is taking you to a land of mysticism.

Lao-tze was a great thinker, but his thoughts were unfathomably deep. You cannot fully understand him. Yet, without fully understanding him, you will be fascinated by him and lured on by his attractions. In the musing of the mystic you can hear music in the air which will quicken your intellect, captivate your imagination and, in its own mystic way, lead you to high mental elevations where in your mind you seem to see things unseen before. He will entertain you almost like a magician on the stage. He juggles with thoughts and ideas in a way which will leave you sometimes utterly bewildered, not knowing exactly what to say and what to believe. To use his own phraseology, you will be sure that he was "a wise merchant," but that he was also one "who hides his treasures"; you will feel that he was "a noble man of perfect virtue," but also one who appeared "as if he were poor" and "as though he were stupid." You will not understand him very much; but you will want very much to understand him.

One thing, however, is quite sure: no matter how critical you are, you will at least feel that he has taught you one great truth—namely, that Truth is Infinite while your mind is finite, and that it is

145

futile for the finite to try to fully comprehend the Infinite. At best we know only in part, and therefore can prophesy only in part; we see truth only through a glass, not face to face. To express it in more Chinese style, how can we see the magnitude of the heavens when we are looking at the sky above while sitting at the bottom of a deep well? How can we measure the vastness of the ocean when all we can do is to dip water with an oyster shell into a little bucket?

Now, is this mysticism or is it realism? Is this metaphysics or is it practical common sense? Would we dare to boast and say that we know, or shall we be moderate and say that we only seek to know? If this is true in dealing with the ordinary and commonplace, how much more so when we are trying to deal with the fundamentals and absolutes? Has any human being yet so fully comprehended the *Tao*, the Eternal Absolute Truth, as to be able to assert with confidence and positiveness that the constant, invariable *Tao* is this and that, or thus and so, and to give it a final definition or name which can forever remain unchanged and unmodified?

In this mysticism we find both repulsion and attraction—repulsion because of the hopelessness of perfect understanding, and attraction because of the unlimited possibilities of an ever-growing ap-

146

prehension of the unsearchable riches. Truth is not
a treasure trove which, when once discovered, is
completely found, and which, when once secured,
is completely possessed. The great truth about it is
that, at least as far as the human apprehension of it
is concerned, Truth is by nature a living organism.
It grows; certainly it grows upon our understanding of it. The seeker of Truth is always on the
road of unending progress, "growing from knowledge to knowledge and from faith to faith." To
use a mathematical metaphor, the process of knowledge is a variable approaching a limit. Truth is
the limit. Our knowledge of Truth is the variable.
We can get closer and closer to the limit, but we
can never fully reach it. The Truth, like all great
laws in the moral or spiritual world, can never be
so framed and defined that it can stand forever unchanged throughout all changes of time and circumstance. *Tao* cannot be defined, and given its
final expression once for all. That which can
be defined, and is defined, is not the constant, invariable, and unchanging *Tao*, or the Truth. No
book is forever up-to-date. New editions probably have to be issued now and then as time changes
and knowledge advances. Therefore, do you not
think that this mystic said something wonderfully
true when he taught that the full apprehension and
final expression of *Tao*, the Truth, is always yet

to be; that we have no right to be too cocksure; and that it is always the part of wisdom not to be too dogmatic?

Now what is this *Tao*, which is the essence as well as the sum and substance of Taoism? The Chinese character *Tao* is very difficult to translate. It is a word very extensively used and referred to in all religious and philosophic literature of China. It is used in the Confucian Analects even more often than in the Tao-Teh-King, although naturally each has given to it its own application and meaning.

This word *Tao* is a composite word made up of two Chinese characters: the character *Shou*, meaning "first," "beginning," "head," or "leader," and the character *Chiah*, meaning "to walk," or "to pace." *Tao*, according to the derivation of the word, therefore suggests the idea of the Way or the Path in which we should walk—the number one path of life. It is also very commonly used to mean the Word, the Truth, or the Doctrine. English, German, and French Sinologues have translated it variously—for example, as Reason, Providence, Truth, Virtue, or even God; but these are all interpretations rather than translations. *Tao* primarily designates the true and correct way of life, the Way of Ways in which man ought to walk, to move and have his being, because it is in accordance with the eternal or absolute truth.

Tao is one of the oldest and commonest words used in Chinese literature. It was used long before the rise of Taoism, but it was Taoism which generalized and mystified it, and which brought it to mean not only a practical method of conduct, but also the eternal law of nature and the metaphysical first principle of life.

Thus *Tao* is the absolute law of the universe. It is the "X" in all the algebraic expressions and formulae of the Taoist philosophy of life. It answers and satisfies all equations; but it has no fixed assigned value in the abstract. It is all-pervading and all-commanding, immutable and unalterable. It has no beginning and no end. It never changes; but it witnesses and withstands all changes. It is the essence of all substance and the regulator of all movement. It is sublime and majestic; but it is formless, nameless, and indefinable.

But can we not give it a little more tangible, concrete form; trace its broad outline, even if we cannot fill in all the details? Can we exhibit it in some sort of a substantial body, and not leave it to be merely an illusive phantom, which even the mind cannot grasp in its imagination? Perhaps the best attempt we can make is to characterize *Tao* as the first cause and creative force in Nature, which permeates the universe and which sustains and regulates it (matter, phenomena, life) by its eternal immutable laws. The following passage from the forty-second chapter of the Tao Teh-King may be used as an illustration in support of this interpretation or exposition of the conception of Tao:

Tao begets one. One begets two. Two begets three. Three begets all things. All things are sustained by *Yin* and *Yang*. They attain harmony through the working of the spirit of non-assertion (or emptiness).

At first sight this is all nonsense, pure and simple; but if we substitute the definition or explanation of *Tao* as given above in the equation of the Taoist philosophy of life we can paraphrase the above passage so as to read thus:

Tao, the first cause or creative force in Nature, produces the cosmos, the *Tai Chi* (here we have the "one"). *Tai Chi* produces the *Yin*,[1] the negative or female principle, and *Yang*, the positive or male principle (here are the "two"). From the operations of these two principles of *Yin* and *Yang*, we have heaven,

[1] The Chinese theory of *Yin* and *Yang* not only supplies a universal basis for classification but a fundamental principle of life. Even in the natural or physical world there must be alternative periods of day and night, summer and winter, sunshine and rain, activity and tranquillity, in order that normal life may be possible.

earth, and mankind (here we have the "three"). These three are the fundamental component elements in the universe. Harmony prevails when the spirit of truth pervades and governs all of them.

In his search for the immutable laws of Nature for the regulation of human conduct, Lao-tze was not without companions among the Western philosophers. The early prevalence of the Christian conception of God and his creative activities has eliminated the necessity of finding a first cause or creative force in Nature; but the search for the *Lex Aeterna*, the Eternal Law of Nature, in accordance with which the universe operates, was a frequent subject of inquiry and discussion among Greek philosophers, Roman writers, and early Christian thinkers down through the Scholastic School of the Middle Ages. Thus we find that Thomas Aquinas spoke of a *Lex Aeterna* which is the ordinance of Divine Wisdom by which all things in heaven and earth are governed, and the reason of Divine Wisdom which is regulative and directive of all actions and motives.[2] We read that Hooker said that law has her seat in the bosom of God, whose voice is the harmony of the world.[3] We recall that Cicero spoke of true law as the right reason or agreement with Nature, which is diffused among all

[2] *Summa Theologica* i. 2.
[3] *Ecclesiastical Polity* 16:8.

151

men and which is not one law at Rome and another at Athens, one law today and another hereafter, but it is the same law everlasting and unchangeable. To all these philosophers Lao-tze, if he could have heard them, would have nodded his head in assent and approval.

Lao-tze's conception of the nature and function of *Tao* provides unlimited fascination for the philosophical mind, which delights in soaring into mystical heights of the imaginary world to speculate on the imponderables of Nature and the universe. But for this very same reason, it has no great value for the common, everyday practical relations of human life. And also for this same reason, the practical-minded Chinese said: "Let us follow Confucius, for he leads us somewhere. And let us keep away from the 'grand old boy,' for he may take us up to dizzy heights in his wild flights."

Such being Lao-tze's conception of the nature and function of *Tao*, his guiding principle for life is easy to understand. If *Tao* is the Supreme Law of Nature, then man's part is simply to conform to Nature. In other words, the law of life is just to be natural. Lao-tze's advice to mankind is to understand the *Tao*—that is, to find the Truth—and then to be in harmony with and identified with the *Tao* —that is, to follow the Truth.

Tao is the mighty stream of life, flowing on from

eternity to eternity; and man will find the end of life—peace, happiness, serenity, and bliss—by completely adjusting himself to it and surrendering to it, trusting to this river of life to carry him to life.

Lao-tze's philosophy of life can be best explained in terms of the theory and practice of swimming. I wonder whether we could imagine Lao-tze as having a private swimming pool of his own, where he took a dip every morning as we now take a shower. He certainly seemed to be an expert in swimming. The first lesson in swimming is to know and understand the nature of water, that it has sufficient buoyancy to keep the body up on the surface.[4] To become an expert swimmer, one must know how to let oneself go in water and to give oneself up to it. Effort is never conspicuous in good swimming. Struggling and meaningless exertions are worse than useless. In perfect absence of fear, with great ease and freedom, the expert glides through the water. His strokes are measured and even; his breathing is regular and rhythmic; his mind is perfectly at ease, and his movements are gentle and quiet. There, on the bosom of the water, he relaxes, perhaps lying pillowed on his arms, enjoying the beauty of the quiet blue sky

[4] It may be interesting to note here that the Chinese speak of a good swimmer as one who understands the nature of water.

153

above. What a life! What an enjoyment of life! That is what you get, or hope to get, when you study in the school of Taoism, and finish your graduate work.

The problem of life is to find the stream of life and understand its deep undying current, entrusting yourself to it and giving yourself to it. Quietude and passive adjustment are all that is needed. Strenuous effort and struggle are not necessary, and not called for. Relax, and let go! Your mind will be at ease, and the tension of life will be released. But the moment you struggle—make foolish motions, or take unnecessary action—you are lost. You do not have to do anything to float on Nature. The best action is nonaction. This is Lao-tze's wonderful idea and marvelous doctrine of nonaction as action, and action by nonaction.

Crude as this illustration is, I think it hits the point of Lao-tze's idea of life and his way of living. There is a river of life accessible to all. The problem is to find it and know how to adjust yourself to it.

The whole system of the Taoist philosophy of life is built on three key words: *Tao-Teh*, Nature, and Nonaction. *Tao* is the Truth, the Eternal Law of Nature, which when expressed in deed or action is the *Teh* or virtue. Nature is the *Tzu Jan* (literally translated, the "self-so" or "naturally so"),

154

suggesting the idea of "I am that I am." It is the "is" which was from the beginning. *Wei-Wu-Wei* (action through nonaction) is noninterference with Nature. Since Lao-tze's basic theory was built upon the conception of the Eternal Law of Nature, we may say that his whole philosophy of life can be summed up in three short expressions: (1) to know Nature, (2) to be natural, and (3) to interfere not with Nature. Lao-tze and his disciples would say: "I live, yet not I, but it is the *Tao* which liveth in me"; for in the *Tao* we live, and move, and have our being. Here we can probably very easily find some similarity of ideas between Taoism and Christianity.

In his theory of "being natural" and his belief in "nonaction" Lao-tze thinks he has discovered the true and perfect way of life. He therefore looks with scornful disdain upon the worldly-wise, the busybody, the self-appointed and self-deceived prophets who try to improve on this perfect way by much ado about nothing, which is worse than useless. Lao-tze may be pictured as saying to us or to himself, in the words of the Psalmist: "Why art thou cast down, O my soul? and why art thou disquieted in me? hope thou in Tao [God in the Psalm]; for I shall yet praise him for the help of his countenance." [5]

[5] Ps. 42:5.

155

Lao-tze perhaps was not very far from the Kingdom. We might say that the main trouble with him was that, though he had the frame, he did not have the true picture in the frame. If the Christian God or even the God of the Psalmist had been the picture in the frame, he would more fully have comprehended the Truth, the Way of Life. The trouble with him was that the picture of the Supreme Being which he needed in the center remained too much of an intangible and incomprehensible abstraction.

We would better understand the teachings of Lao-tze and the rise of Taoism if we should bear in mind the age in which Lao-tze lived and the historical background in which Taoism arose. Lao-tze taught in an age of feudal anarchy; and Taoism arose in the days of serious disturbances in the Han Dynasty. What he taught concerning inaction, or, more correctly perhaps, concerning unnatural and undue interference, was a satirical condemnation of the perversion of the ends of law as seen in the harsh and bad laws of the time, which, instead of stabilizing society, maintaining justice, promoting harmony and happiness among men as they ought to do, were, in effect, doing just the opposite. Therefore, the remedy was worse than the malady; and if so, the less of it the better, urged Lao-tze.

The time was out of joint. Before any appreciable improvement could be expected, it was necessary to rejoin the actual with the ideal, the transient with the eternal, the earth with heaven, the human with the divine, the artificial with the natural, the finite with the infinite, the partial with the complete, and the relative with the absolute.

More particularly it was perhaps intended to be a sarcastic criticism of the Confucian School for its insistence and emphasis upon the "Pharisean" meticulous observance of the multifarious rules of propriety. To Lao-tze and his school of thought such efforts were vain and useless; neither the means used nor the ends sought were perfect. There was a better way and a sounder principle—to know Nature, and to conform to it.

Both Confucianism and Taoism looked forward to a Golden Era, a perfect and ideal state, wherein tranquillity and harmony would prevail, and where everybody would be content and happy. But there is this great difference. Taoism conceived it to be the "undegenerated" state of Nature, and centered its thoughts on Nature, and was thus always talking about the fixed, immutable Law of Nature, which man can learn to know but cannot alter or improve. Who by thought or effort can add to his height, or can change the color of a single hair! Confucianism thought in terms of a regenerated state or moral perfection, and centered its thoughts

157

on the man, and believed in the creative effort of man to exalt *Tao* and build up the ideal state. Man is to be co-worker with Nature, call it Providence or God as you like.

The Psalmist said: "When I consider thy heavens, the work of thy fingers, the moon and the stars, which thou hast ordained; what is man, that thou art mindful of him? and the son of man, that thou visitest him?" [6] Confucianism magnified the man, and emphasized his creative power in the world and over Nature, while Taoism minimized the man in the vastness and majesty of Nature. Perhaps both have a useful function to perform, each serving as a check and balance on the other.

The fundamental mistake or fallacy in the Tao philosophy of Lao-tze is in the failure to draw the distinction between man and matter or objects of nature.[7] The two are different, and must live by different rules. Man is a higher creature, living on a higher plane; therefore, he must be governed by higher rules than the rules prevailing and applicable to the world of nature and to the kingdom of animals and plants. Inanimate objects of nature and animals will live, thrive, and grow best when left

[6] Ps. 8:3-4.

[7] This was the criticism of Mr. Liang Chi-chao, who, with Kang Yu-hui, started the Reform Movement of 1898, and was perhaps the most brilliant writer and thinker of the modern era in China.

alone. Any action upon them and interference by
the action of man is always detrimental to their
welfare; left alone in the state of nature, they are
free and unmolested; coming in contact with man,
the trees are chopped down, the horses are bridled,
the oxen are yoked, and the fish are caught. They
would all live longer and be freer and happier—if
we can imagine objects of nature as capable of such
feeling—were man to leave them to nature without
any interference.

But man is different. We cannot leave him entirely to his nature and unrestricted free will; if we
do we shall see him treading upon somebody's
toes, infringing upon somebody else's freedom, and
interfering with somebody else's rights. The Uto-
pia of Lao-tze, on the basis of his "back to Nature"
philosophy, is only possible when man lives in
seclusion or in primordial small groups, not extending beyond the family or village. Indeed, the
Tao-Teh-King[8] pictures the good old days when
men, in their primordial simplicity, lived in such
close proximity to each other as to be able to hear
the crow of the cock in one village and the barking
of the dog in another village; yet they were so
self-contented in a happy self-contained life that
they did not exchange visits from one village to

[8] Tao-Teh-King lxxx.

another throughout their whole life. Beautiful picture of splendid isolation! But gone forever are such good old days, if indeed they ever actually existed or could possibly have existed at any time.

To the logical mind and sociable nature of the Chinese such a theory and such a system appears to be too fantastic and unreal. Thus the "grand old boy," though undoubtedly an intellectual giant —maybe even more of an intellectual giant than Confucius—did not draw as large a following. The Utopian society of Lao-tze may be ideally perfect and beautiful, but it is just too good to be true. Our legs of faith or imagination are too short to make such a high jump. Shall we say that Confucius planted his feet on the ground and then tried to hitch his wagon to the star and pull it toward heaven, while Lao-tze tried to jump to the star first and then to haul the wagon to heaven.

Lao-tze, however, did have certain very important contributions to make to the philosophy of life, which were both valuable and original. But in general it may be said that his philosophy is stimulating rather than instructive, suggestive rather than authoritative. In endeavoring to correct some of the extreme views of his time and age, Lao-tze perhaps laid himself much more open to the criticism of being guilty of overstatements and extreme views. In his Tao-Teh-King we find many sparkling gems of great value, but they are too often still embedded in uncut stones and are thus unextracted and only partially seen. There are, however, thoughts which are truly profound, and teachings which are really instructive, some of which may be briefly mentioned.

1. *His majestic conception of the Tao.* His discourse on the nature of *Tao* excites the imagination and produces an unquenchable thirst; one is moved to press on continuously to seek greater and greater light, to know more and more of the Truth, which constitutes the Ultimate Reality in the universe. One cannot read the Tao-Teh-King without getting the impression that *Tao* is majestic and magnificent, immeasurable in its magnitude, unfathomable in its depth, boundless in its width, unsearchable in its richness, eternal and immutable. To this his great disciple Chuang-tze, the "Mencius of Taoism," added the quality of poetic beauty, with resounding notes setting in motion unending echoes of melody. In his discourse on *Tao*, Laotze places before us an infinite objective, which we can never fully understand, but which we would ever seek to know; so we press on and on, ever broadening our vision the higher we advance, continually widening the horizon, as a person going up from deck to deck in a ship on the ocean, admiring the vast expanse of the boundless deep.

Therefore, let us sing with the New England poet:

> Build thee more stately mansions, O my soul,
> As the swift seasons roll!
> Leave thy low-vaulted past!
> Let each new temple, nobler than the last,
> Shut thee from heaven with a dome more vast,
> Till thou at length art free,
> Leaving thine outgrown shell by life's unresting
> sea! [9]

Forward and onward let us press, seeking continual growth in knowledge and understanding, to comprehend and to be comprehended of the Truth.

2. *Warning against an overconfidence in any human scheme of life.* Another important contribution of Lao-tze is his teaching that the center of life and the fountain of wisdom are not in man but in something somewhere beyond the man. To him the confidence, or rather the overconfidence, placed in any humanly devised perfect scheme of life is unjustifiable. Let the wise man be humble; and let him turn to *Tao*, the Infinite, for guidance and support. *Tao* gives us the only fixed pattern and standard for reference. All other foundations on which we attempt to build an ideal and permanent structure for life are but sinking earth and shifting sand. Self-reliance is necessary; but overconfidence

[9] From Oliver Wendell Holmes's "The Chambered Nautilus."

is dangerous. The canopy of material civilization which we set over our head, no matter how beautiful it is, and how much pride we take in it, may be found actually to be an easily torn leaking roof under which we are seeking shelter. The idol which we have so carefully fashioned with such artificial genius, and which we have set up to worship, may be a golden image; but, after all, it is a man-made idol with clay feet, ready to tumble down at any moment under stress. This "grand old man" of China is calling upon mankind to "stop, look, and listen," as it so confidently swings along on the road of material civilization with bold strides and marching band.

3. *Some of his ethical teachings are very remarkable*. This is perhaps best illustrated by his teaching about overcoming evil with good, although his denunciation of war, and his call to a life of simplicity, and his doctrine of quietude, all contain much food for thought.

> To those who are good, I am good.
> To those who are not good, I am also good.
> For, goodness is virtue.
> To those who are faithful, I am faithful.
> To those who are not faithful, I am also faithful.
> For, faithfulness is virtue.[10]

[10] Tao-Teh-King xlix.

163

Meet hatred with virtue (or kindness).[11]

Such sayings are perhaps as close to the Christian conception of love as can be found in any other non-Christian religion.[12]

The whole Confucian social philosophy was built upon the principle of justice and righteousness; it exhorts every man to give every other man his just due. That will give human society stability. But the idea of meeting evil with good is a distinct contribution of Lao-tze. It introduced a broader principle of life—one which will not only facilitate and accelerate the kingdom of righteousness and justice which Confucianism strived to attain, but will give man greater happiness and deeper satisfaction all around. Justice tempered with love and love coupled with justice is virtue in due proportion and proper balance. It is an ideal combination for a life; it is a healthy and well-balanced principle for the promotion of social welfare and social progress. Some such perfect fulfillment of the law and the prophets may be found when Confucianism and the Taoism of Lao-tze meet and grasp each other.

4. *Hidden meaning and deeper truths.* One

[11] Tao-Teh-King lxiii.

[12] The most outstanding "disciple of love" among the old Chinese philosophers was of course Mo-tze, whose great theme was love for all alike.

feature of outstanding significance of the Tao-Teh-King is the many paradoxical statements which it contains. Many of these choice gems are similar in form as well as in spirit to such Biblical statements as "the meek . . . . shall inherit the earth," [13] and "He that findeth his life shall lose it: and he that loseth his life for my sake shall find it." [14] The following are some samples:

Tao appears to be inactive, yet it is active in all things.[15]

Great success may appear like failure, but its effect persists;

Great fulness may appear like emptiness, but its use is inexhaustible.

Great straightness may appear crooked; great skill may seem clumsy; and great eloquence may sound like stammering.[16]

Seeing the most tender (weakness) overriding the most hard (strongest),

And the immaterial entering the impenetrable,

I thereby understand the advantage of "non-action" or "non-assertion." [17]

Faithful words may not be pleasant; pleasant words may not be faithful.

[13] Matt. 5:5.
[14] Matt. 10:39.
[15] Tao-Teh-King xxxvii.
[16] Tao-Teh-King xlv.
[17] Tao-Teh-King xliii.

The good (or well-informed) are not contentious;
    the contentious are not good.
The wise is not necessarily learned; the learned is not
    necessarily wise.
The holy man hoards not: for, the more he does not
    for others, the more he himself owns; the more
    he gives to others, the more he himself acquires.
The way of Heaven is to benefit and not to injure;
The way of the holy man is to serve and not to con-
    tend.[18]

It can be seen easily, even from the few samples
given above, that many of the sayings of Lao-tze
contain important elements of truth in them; but
they are not "the whole truth and nothing but the
truth." They have to be sifted, or put through
a refinery. But there is one very important contribution he has made. He has taught the great
truth, which a thoughtful person will probably in-
variably get from reading through the Tao-Teh-
King, that beneath the ideals accepted as truths
in the current thinking of men there are yet greater
and deeper truths, which we should seek to find
and understand.

III. TAOISM AS A RELIGION

We have seen that Taoism as a religion is historically related to, but in teaching quite different

[18] Tao-Teh-King lxxxi.

from, Taoism as a philosophy. As a philosophy it is one of very high order, although speculative and mystic. As a religion in actual practice, however, it is of a rather low form, full of idolatry and superstition. In China it is the religion of the unlearned and ignorant, while Confucianism and Buddhism, comparatively speaking, are religions of the learned and cultured. However, even though its practices are full of superstitions, there are elements of value in it.

The central objective of Taoism is to discover the way to immortality, just as the central idea of Buddhism is to find a way of escape from the sufferings of life. The Taoist idea of immortality is, however, merely everlasting life. It is essentially an indefinite prolongation of the present earthly existence. The Taoist immortals are supposed to enjoy freedom or liberation from the restrictions of time and space, and to have an unending innocent happy life—as it were, in an everlasting kindergarten of happiness.

A very popular presentation of the idea of immortality is found in the story of the famous Eight Immortals, or Eight Fairies, as they are sometimes called. It is well known and very popular in China. These Eight Fairies are seen in paintings, in curios or objects of art, and are often made into small gold or silver figures used for decorations on hats

167

worn by the children. They are particularly made use of, in one form or another, in giving birthday presents. The story is part of the Chinese mythology often referred to in poetry and literature.

The composition of this group of Fairies is exceedingly interesting, containing one official, one scholar, one doctor, one lame beggar, one youth, one woman, one musician, etc. In other words, rich and poor, high and low, men and women, young and old, are all represented in it—a very cosmopolitan and very democratic group.[19] They

[19] The story of the Eight Immortal Fairies originated with the Yuan Dynasty, between the thirteenth and fourteenth centuries, but has become very popular and widely known. These "Eight Happy Immortals" were:

1. *Han Chung-li*, who was the doyen of this Corps of Immortals. He would always be pictured as carrying a *fan*, with which he could revive the spirit of the dead. (Each of these Eight Fairies could be identified by a particular instrument or article which he or she always carried about.)

2. *Chang Kuo-lao*, legendary figure who lived to great age. He was said to be a renowned magician, well versed in necromancy. He would always be pictured carrying a *bamboo tap drum*, often be found riding on a paper donkey, which could carry him one thousand miles a day, but which he could fold up and put in his wallet when not in use.

3. *Han Hsiang-tze*, who was the nephew of the celebrated Chinese scholar, *Han Yu*. He was the "Happy Youth" of the party. Once, by dashing a cup of wine on the ground, he produced a bouquet, with a character on each flower, producing a beautiful poem. He would always be pictured carrying a *flute*. He has been regarded as the patron saint of the musicians.

168

live in the enjoyment of innocent pleasure, but occasionally they interest themselves in helping some poor helpless mortal.

The Taoist Pantheon has many gods, some of them also very interesting. At the top of the list is the *Yu Huang* or Jade Emperor, the creator of heaven and earth as well as of man. Lao-tze is

4. *Tieh Kwah-li*, who was of the gentry and a philosopher. He would always be pictured as a lame beggar, leaning on an *iron staff*, because, it was said, on one of the celestial trips he was in the habit of taking, his disciples had thought him dead and had burned his body, so he had to take refuge in the body of a poor beggar who had just died.

5. *Tsao Kuo-chiu*, who was the brother-in-law of one of the emperors of the Sung Dynasty. He was therefore a *mandarin*, a high official among the nobility. He would always be pictured carrying a *pair of flappers* in his hand, as he has been regarded as the patron saint of the dramatists.

6. *Li Tsung-ping*, who was a *Han-lin* scholar (one of those holding the highest academic degrees), and a doctor by profession. It was said that he had tasted all kinds of herbs in order to discover their medicinal properties. He would always be pictured carrying a *sword*, with which he could drive off evil monsters.

7. *Ho Hsien-kuo*, "the Maiden Immortal," who was the daughter of a shopkeeper. She lived on powdered mother of pearls and moonbeams, which diet produced immortality. She would always be pictured carrying a *lotus flower*, the emblem of loveliness and purity.

8. *Lan Ts'ai-ho*, who was the myth of the myths, as the story did not tell whether this immortal was man or woman, nor the when and where of living. (But, what of it, when we deal with immortality!) This fairy was usually pictured as a woman, with one foot shod and one foot bare, carrying a *flower basket*.

169

regarded as the incarnation of the *Yu Huang*. Of the rest, perhaps the two most interesting ones are the City God and the Kitchen God.

In almost every city there is a City Temple in which is found the City God. The arrangement of the City Temple is very interesting in that, we may say, it is planned on the best psychological principles. As soon as a person steps in, he will, unexpectedly but almost immediately, run into such signboards or notices as "Ah, here you come also. Just looking for you. All good will be rewarded; and all evil must be punished." In the main hall of the temple he will probably find, exhibited in a prominent way, a great abacus, or Chinese counting board (China's old-style adding and calculating machine), a vivid and sharp reminder that the day of reckoning is at hand. This abacus expresses the Taoist theory of life as the lotus flower expresses the Buddhist theory. But the pre-eminent thing is that the City Temple serves as a standing reminder that, as there is a natural law in the natural world, so there is a spiritual law in the spiritual world, and that sooner or later we must leave this natural world to go to the spiritual world and settle our "account" for the doings of this life, receiving reward for good deeds done and punishment for evils committed.

The Kitchen God is the guardian of the family.

170

If in some popular Christian customs a kindly Santa Claus is supposed to come down the chimney to the family to bring Christmas gifts for the children, in Chinese Taoism the Kitchen God sits in a niche in the chimney all the year round, as the silent guest and unseen supervisor. Only once a year, also at about Christmas time, he departs to heaven to make his annual report of the merits and demerits of the family and its members.

Although Taoism, as a religion, is not held in high esteem, there are points at which it may supplement both Confucianism and Buddhism in giving to the Chinese a more rounded view of life. On the whole we may say that Confucianism is too serious and formal; Buddhism, too resigned and pessimistic; but that Taoism, in spite of its superstitions, gives a touch of bright color to an otherwise too somber view of life.

In at least three things Taoism makes a distinct contribution to the Chinese view of life:

1. It is the only religion of China which gives a prominent place to physical culture. Buddhism regards the body as excess baggage, a hindrance and stumbling block to spiritual growth. Confucianism does not ignore it; for filial piety demands that we take good care of the body which we receive from our parents; and a thorough education, in order to be complete, must include archery and

171

charioteering. But, in practice, physical culture has always been subordinate to intellectual training, so that in China the old-type scholar usually had bad eyesight and feeble muscles. The scholar, by his weak physique and strong intellect, was China's declaration of faith that in intellectual culture, and not in physical force, lies the strength and confidence of the nation. To the Taoist, however, who seeks everlasting life, the body is the basis and starting point for his immortal life. He is to be careful with his mode of living, avoiding all sorts of excess and dissipation and developing good habits of dieting and breathing, which is the way of the internal culture of the "pill of immortality."

2. It was in time past an important factor in the promotion of social service and community improvement. Taoism directs one's attention to the accumulation of merits through good deeds. One way of acquiring such merits is through making contributions for paving the streets and building bridges. This custom served a very useful and practical purpose in those days when such public works were not regarded as municipal or government functions. The Taoists were not the only ones promoting such activities, but they were perhaps the most active. Buddhists would more likely contribute money to building or repairing temples and giving the images of gods therein a new coat

of gilt. But the Taoist would be disposed to do such good social acts as would be credited to his account of merit. Popular Taoism regards the course of life as a course in strict accounting; he who has a large enough balance in good deeds and merits in the book of life will receive the reward of life.[20] It is the Boy Scout idea of "one good deed each day," extended and expanded. The roads and bridges were the monuments of social philanthropy in old China. So, every time you go through the beautiful arch of a Chinese bridge you see therein a "Carnegie Library" or a "Rockefeller Institute" and the hope and faith of somebody that a unit was thereby added on the abacus recording the accumulated merit of his life.

3. But the greatest distinct contribution of Taoism to the life ideas of China is its cheerful, even though it may appear too playful, outlook upon life. Confucianism is all work and no play; life is dignified but stiff. But in the picture of the Eight Immortals we have a mythological story which, believe it or not, takes us out on the wings of fancy

[20] For a fuller presentation of this view, read the *Tai-Shang Kang-Ying Pien*, known in English as *Tractate of Actions and Their Retributions* or *Book of Rewards and Punishments*. Literally, the two Chinese words *Kang-Ying* mean "to stimulate response." In other words, the central thought of this Taoist tractate is that the condition of our life is just the reaction stimulated by our actions, good or bad.

173

for a holiday excursion to a fairy island in the Eastern Sea.[21] The Buddhist says, Life is all suffering and tears; so let us get out of it as soon and as completely as possible. Taoism says, Life is good and worth living; let us improve it and prolong it indefinitely.

Through the counting board to the happy fairy land! This is the Taoist message to mankind. It is its patented formula for the manufacture of the "pill of immortality" and the elixir of life. *Bon voyage* and all success. This is the Taoist blessing upon you!

[21] It is very interesting to note that in China, the "Land of Supreme Happiness" (*Chi-Lo-Kuo*), the Buddhist Paradise, is said to be located in Western Heaven; while the Isle of the Immortal Fairies (*Peng-Lai-Tao*), the Taoist Paradise, is said to be located in the Eastern Sea. There is thus not even any conflict in the geographical location of these two happy lands.

174

CHRISTIANITY: THE WAY OF LIFE

As we have seen from the preceding chapters, China has had perhaps more than a due share of the religions of the world. China has had Confucianism; China has had Buddhism; and China has had Taoism. Yet, in spite of this rich cultural heritage, there is not found in these religions that which can really quench the thirst of the soul and give man that spiritual dynamic for an abounding life. Such, indeed, is always the case, either with an individual or with a nation, in whose heart the spirit of Christ moves not.

"I am the true vine, and my Father is the husbandman. . . . . He that abideth in me, and I in him, the same bringeth forth much fruit. . . . . If a man abide not in me, he is cast forth as a branch, and is withered." [1] These things have been spoken to us that the real joy of life may remain in us and that our joy may be full. These words are true and faithful, and faithful and true is He who said them.

[1] John 15:1-6.

Each of the founders of "the three religions of China" has his contribution to make, to China and perhaps to the world also. But neither Confucius, nor Buddha, nor Lao-tze, each by himself alone, or all three of them acting together, can give to China, or any other nation, that which only the living, life-giving Christ Jesus can give—the living water which can make him who drinketh never become thirsty again. He and he alone is the Way of Life. He and he alone can give to man that abundant life, even the life eternal.

What is life eternal? It is a life which is not only eternal in length, but also in height, in breadth, and in depth. It is eternal in length, for our Lord saith: "Because I live, ye shall live also";[2] "In my Father's house are many mansions. . . . . I go to prepare a place for you."[3] It is eternal in height, because "as many as received him, to them gave he power to become the sons of God."[4] We Christians are called to be "perfect, even as [our] Father which is in heaven is perfect."[5] It is eternal in breadth, because we are to love all men as our neighbors and all neighbors as ourselves; we are to feel ourselves as a part of whole humanity, mem-

[2] John 14:19.
[3] John 14:2.
[4] John 1:12.
[5] Matt. 5:48.

176

bers of the universal brotherhood of man under the universal fatherhood of God; and we are to identify ourselves with the need and aspirations of man and mankind as the Son of Man did. It is eternal in depth, because we are to be in touch and in communion with the universal Divine Power which quickens the soul, which creates in us a new heart, and which brings forth a new man through being born again in the Holy Spirit.

To the unconverted and unredeemed, this is strange doctrine indeed. "The wind bloweth where it listeth, and thou hearest the sound thereof, but canst not tell whence it cometh, and whither it goeth: so is every one that is born of the Spirit." [6] We may not be able to explain all the mystery involved in it; but we can see the effect of it. It may be a mystery; but it is a reality. We speak of what we do know, and testify of that we have seen.

Every nation has its "father Jacob" and "his well"; but for all countries and all lands there has been only one who has given us the living water which can give complete and perfect satisfaction. Every age has its own prophets—John the Baptist, the reformer; Elias, the seer; Jeremiah, the patriot—but throughout all ages there has been only one Christ—the Christ who is the Son of God, on the

[6] John 3:8.

177

one hand, and who is the Son of Man, for all man and mankind, on the other. This is he who only is the Lamb of God that taketh away the sin of the world, and this is he who only is the begotten Son of God, whom God has given to the world out of his love, "that whosoever believeth in him should not perish, but have everlasting life." [7] He alone is our Redeemer and Saviour. "In him was life; and the life was the light of men." [8]

Ask the Confucianist in China whether he is fully satisfied; I am sure he will say "No." Ask the Buddhist in China whether he is fully satisfied; I am sure he will also say "No." Ask the Taoist the same question; and you will get the same answer. There can be no uncertainty; none of them is fully satisfied. They are all still in search of the living faith which can lead to life eternal; they know that they have not found it yet. "To whom shall we go?" they are all asking.

This absence of full satisfaction is due not only to the consciousness of failure of personal effort or lack of individual attainment; it is also due to a realization that what they have put their trust in is itself imperfect and inefficient. That each of these religions has some merit, we can readily concede; but that each of them has its own very serious

[7] John 3:16.
[8] John 1:4.

178

and apparent limitations, even their most ardent advocates or devotees will likely admit. They are all broken beams of light and fragmentary segments of the whole.

Even as philosophies of life they all leave much to be desired. Confucianism is too humanistic, and so is one-sided, lacking in comprehensiveness. It deals only with human relations in this life. But no real thinking man can be entirely unaware of the great "beyond" when he is in a mood of deep meditation and quiet reflection. In his consciousness of the magnitude of life and the vastness of time and the universe, he cannot feel convinced or be satisfied that this brief earthly span of a few scores of years is the sum total of his complete life, and that his social contacts with his fellow men exhaust all his relations in the vast eternity of time and space.

Buddhism is too pessimistic—in mood, in spirit, and in outlook. Man surely is more than just a mote in the sunbeam, or a trifling toy in the hands of Fate. There is much more for man to do than to seek a way of escape and lose himself in a vacuum. "To be, or not to be," that indeed is the question; but for Buddhism it is a question of "Which is the worse?" not "Which is the better?" Buddha was no great spiritual physician who could restore man to radiant spiritual health, so that he

179

could experience the joy of living. At best, what Buddhism can do is to administer an injection of anesthetic so that one may become insensible and unconscious of pain and suffering; but such anesthesia does not remove the cause of pain itself. Buddha was not the kind of Great Physician we Christians see in our Lord Jesus Christ.

Taoism is too fantastic. You may wander with Lao-tze in the realm of imagination, dreaming perhaps with his great disciple Chuang-tze that you are a butterfly fluttering from flower to flower, enjoying the free air and the beauty of nature, and for a moment so losing yourself in philosophic mysticism that you are not sure whether it is you dreaming yourself a butterfly or a butterfly dreaming itself as you; [9] but when you wake to life's realities, the hard and stern facts of existence will still be with you. In your dream you may imagine yourself as having climbed a ladder leading high up to heaven, but when you awaken you will still find your head resting on the stones for a pillow.

None of the three has found the real way of full salvation, either for himself or for mankind. Con-

---

[9] This "Butterfly Dream" is one of the most famous passages in the whole book of Chuang-tze. It is a good illustration both of his mysticism and of his fascinating style. The passage is found in *Sacred Books of the East*, Volume XXXIX, page 197.

fucius did not go far enough, having confined himself to the immediate without touching the ultimate. Buddha lost his way before reaching the end, not knowing whether to affirm or deny the ultimate existence of either the self or the soul, and not sure of what Nirvana really is. Lao-tze did not have a solid foundation. The *Tao*, upon which his whole system and philosophy of life is built, is nameless and inexplicable, and so is incomprehensible and intangible. He was indeed trying to build a beautiful air castle on a foundation of shifting sand.

Each of them, be it acknowledged, tried to describe a complete circle for life; but each of them failed in some respect. Confucius used too short a radius and made the circle too small for the complete development of the "full man." Buddha projected too much into uncertainties, and got so hopelessly tangled up in inextricable complications and inconsistencies that even he himself could not clearly trace the circumference. Lao-tze might have been a very skillful draftsman; but, having no fixed center to start with, he could never complete the circle.

Only Jesus Christ presents the complete circle. He is the Way, the Truth, and the Life. In him are all three to find their fulfillment and realization. Because he is the Way, the Taoists can only have a real, firm grasp on the *Tao* when they have com-

181

prehended him. Because he is the Truth, the Buddhists can only have the great illumination and awakening for which they are ever seeking in vain when they have come into his light—the light which lighteth every man that cometh into the world. Because he is the Life, the Confucianists can only have an adequate knowledge of the true objective of living and the actual experience of the fullness of life when they have come to follow him and to learn to live his life.

Christianity is unique. It is not only the faith for the living, but a living faith—a faith in which all men can find, not only light, but life itself, and whereby all persons may live most aboundingly. Christianity is the only real Gospel because it is not only an "ism" or an "ology," but is the power of God unto salvation. Christianity is the only adequate Gospel because at the center of our circle of life is the living Christ, who is able to save, and who is the same yesterday, today, and forever.

> O grant us light, that we may learn
>   How dead is life from Thee apart,
> How sure is joy for all who turn
>   To Thee an undivided heart.[10]

It is for this reason that Christianity as a religion is peerless and matchless. Christianity is not only

[10] Lawrence Tuttiett.

182

the best philosophy for life, but the life of the best philosophy. Our Christ is not only one who teaches and preaches, but one who lives, serves, and saves. All the other religions of the world have certain food values for a man's spiritual and moral development, but every one of them is at the same time deficient in certain essential vitamins. They all have certain points which are quite similar to the teachings of Christianity; but they all fall far below the requirement for a complete, full salvation either for the individual man or for the whole of mankind; and in the final analysis the other religions are even without a completely satisfactory theory of life.

I. TAOISM AND CHRISTIANITY

Let us first consider Taoism. In its conception of the sublimity of *Tao* it comes very close to the Christian concept of the "Logos." In the following passage from the Gospel of John: "In the beginning was the Word, and the Word was with God, and the Word was God. The same was in the beginning with God. All things were made by him; and without him was not any thing made that was made. In him was life; and the life was the light of men," we may insert the word *Tao* in place of the word "Word" and incorporate it into any commentary on the philosophy of *Tao*,

183

without producing a note of discord. In fact, in the Chinese translation of the Bible, the English "Word" or the Greek "Logos" has been translated *Tao;* so the first sentence of the Gospel according to St. John would read, if we should translate it back to English, "In the beginning was *Tao,* and *Tao* was with God, and *Tao* was God."

But there is this great difference. In Taoism, this *Tao* is impersonal and incomprehensible, vague and elusive. In Christianity, it is a living personality, the expression of God's divine love and redeeming grace, and the manifestation of man's highest possibilities. He is so real and so close to us that, if we would completely surrender our lives to him, we could say, "In him we live, and move, and have our being"; we could also feel as Paul did: "I live; yet not I, but Christ liveth in me."

Again, we may say that in the idea of immortality there is also a point of great similarity between Taoism and Christianity, yet here again there are some fundamental differences. We may point out an essential difference by saying that immortality in Taoism is merely a continuing everlasting life, while in Christianity, as we have seen, it is eternal life— with a richness and fullness of meaning of which we are not often fully aware. Taoist immortality is essentially an indefinite prolongation of the present earthly existence. The Taoist immortals are supposed to enjoy freedom or liberation from the restrictions of time and space, and an unending innocent happy life. However pleasant such a life may be, it is lacking in fullness and completeness, without deep meaning and high purpose. The Christian idea of immortality is a life eternal—not only an unending existence, but also one of unlimited development in spiritual richness and fullness.

II. BUDDHISM AND CHRISTIANITY

Let us take up Buddhism next. When we make a comparison between Buddhism and Christianity, at least the following points of similarity and dissimilarity are worthy of note.

1. *As to the Problem of Evil in the World.* To the Buddhist, the great problem of evil in the world is the experience of suffering. Therefore, the great quest is, how to eliminate suffering. To the Christian, the problem of evil includes the problem of sin; there is suffering because there is sin. Death, the greatest and the inescapable suffering, is the wages of sin. Buddhism does not ignore the relationship between sin and suffering; but its major emphasis and primary concern is simply on the fact of suffering. Sin is to be eradicated because that is the only way to eliminate suffering. Christianity, on the other hand, faces suffering primarily as a

185

consequence of sin. Its primary concern is the elimination of sin, which will automatically relieve man of his suffering.

2. *As to the Way of Salvation.* In this connection there is a difference both in respect to the ends sought and the means employed. As to the first, it has already been pointed out that Buddhism seeks chiefly a way of escape from the miseries of life, while Christianity is much more positive because it strives to secure victory over sin. The distinction here is the difference between the defeatist mood and the triumphant spirit.

As to the second, the means to be employed in achieving the end, Buddhism stresses the importance of Enlightenment, finding the Truth which will set man free; while Christianity emphasizes getting the new life through Jesus Christ, the life which is also the light of man. Whenever we read of the Buddhist discourse on Light and Enlightenment, our minds almost instinctively run to the first chapter of the Gospel according to St. John, where he discusses the light and life of man. Superficially it would seem that the teaching in Buddhism is very similar to the exposition in John's Gospel. Upon careful examination it is clear, however, that there is an important difference, in that Buddhism considers that light is the life of men whereas what the Bible teaches is that "the life [is] the light of men."

186

Christian teaching is fully true, while the Buddhist conception is only partially true. Light is knowledge. Knowledge is an important element in life; but it is not life itself. A certain kind of life will always bring along with it the light or knowledge pertaining to that life; but the converse is not always true. A circus trainer or stage performer may know all about his monkey or sea lion, and the monkey or sea lion so trained may know a good deal about the man; but this knowledge will not make the man a monkey or the monkey a man. Thus also, moral life will always bring along with it knowledge of morality; but mere knowledge of morality will not always bring along with it moral life. If a man will do God's will, he shall know of the doctrine; but not everyone who saith, "Lord, Lord," shall enter into the Kingdom. Life brings light of knowledge; but light of knowledge does not necessarily bring life.

3. *As to the Conception of Life.* According to Buddhism,

> Life is but an empty dream!— ....
> And things are not what they seem.[11]

But according to Christianity,

> Life is real! Life is earnest!
> And the grave is not its goal! [12]

[11] From Longfellow's "A Psalm of Life."
[12] *Ibid.*

In Buddhism everything is transient, unreal, and nonexistent. To the devout Buddhist, life is, at best, quiet and tranquil; but it is melancholic and pessimistic. To the Christian, life is full of confidence, joy, and triumph. The most that the Buddhist can hope to achieve is peace of heart; but the Christian can, in addition, look to the joy which God gives, and which no man can take away.

4. *As to the Conception of God.* Buddhism started out with no god; but it ends having too many gods. It started out having no place for prayer; but it ends with attributing too much value to the mere repetition of the words of prayer. In Buddhism, all persons are like the "man without a country," wandering about fatherless and homeless. In Christianity, Jesus Christ revealed to us that God is not only righteous and just, but he is to us also a loving Father. In Buddhism, God and his ways are unfathomably deep or hopelessly hazy. In Christianity, God and his eternal laws are not only inexhaustibly rich and infinitely inspiring; but they are, at the same time, so plain and easily understood that they may be as real to the children as they are to the aged, and as meaningful to the simple as they are to the wise. When Jesus was only twelve years old he could say, "Wist ye not that I must be about my Father's business?"

5. *As to the Conception of Prayer.* Buddhism

lays great emphasis on meditation. This practice is of course very similar to, and has much the same purpose as, the Christian practice of prayer. But there is perhaps this very important difference. In Buddhist meditation the central objective and main effort is to empty the mind of evil thoughts—in the most perfect form, of all thoughts whatsoever. This is both the experiment and the cultivation for Nirvana. Christian prayer differs from the Buddhist meditation in at least two important respects: (1) the Christian prayer is not simply to empty one's mind of all thoughts, but to fill it with thoughts about God, not just to forget or eliminate oneself, but to enter into spiritual fellowship with him and to learn to live in his presence; and (2) it is not only supplication for oneself, as the Buddhist is, but for others as well, and particularly for the coming of God's Kingdom. The Buddhist practice is simply a bleaching process to remove the stain of sin and evil, but the Christian prayer involves the stamping of the image of Christ on the mind of the worshiper. The Buddhist prayer cleans the spark plugs, but the Christian prayer charges the battery with power for action.

III. Confucianism and Christianity

There is very little in the teachings of Confucius which is contradictory to the teachings of Jesus

189

Christ. But Christianity deals with the problems of life much more fully and much better. The proper Christian attitude toward Confucianism is therefore one of "fulfillment," and not one of "destruction." Confucius may be conceived as the voice of a prophet crying in the Far East: "Prepare ye the way of the Lord, make his paths straight; for the kingdom of heaven is at hand." Confucianism, by exalting virtue, emphasizing the spiritual values of life, teaching the principle of benevolence and due regard for others, expressing faith in and respect for a Supreme Deity, etc., has given the Chinese people much spiritual preparation which Christianity can well utilize in its presentation of Jesus Christ the Saviour, and his Gospel of the Kingdom of God.

Among the outstanding points of similarity and common emphasis which Confucianism shares with Christianity, the following may be mentioned.

1. *Appreciation of the Spiritual Values in Life.* In both there is an appreciation that there are some things—ideals, principles, spiritual assets—which are more real, more important, and more valuable than life itself. Jesus Christ said: "But seek ye first the kingdom of God, and his righteousness." [13] Confucius said that a "princely man seeks after Truth (*Tao*) more than food"—that is, his material needs—

[13] Matt. 6:33.

and that "if a man hears the Truth in the morning, he may die in the evening without regret."[14] Mencius said: "Life I desire, but there is that which I desire more than life; death I detest, but there is that which I detest more than death."[15]

2. *Devotion to Truth and Righteousness.* Both teach that devotion to truth and righteousness is the supreme pursuit of life. According to the Confucian teaching, the supreme object of living is to be righteous. Even more than "to know thyself," life's supreme injunction is "to be thyself"—to be true to your best, at all times and under all circumstances; even in solitude or in obscurity, when nobody sees you or takes note of you;[16] and even in barbarous and uncivilized communities, when people neither appreciate nor admire you.[17] "What a princely man is he, who, when unrecognized (of his virtue or attainment), yet harbours no resentment!"[18]

3. *Theory of the Stewardship of Life.* Both uphold the theory of the stewardship of life. The Confucian theory is that kings and teachers are constituted by Heaven to be leaders and guides of

[14] Analects xv. 31 and iv. 8.
[15] Mencius, Bk. II. Pt. I. x. 2.
[16] Great Learning vi. 2.
[17] Analects xv. 5.
[18] Analects i.

the people.[19] Therefore their talents and position are given to them with a divine commission to be used in the service of their fellow men. "For unto whomsoever much is given, of him shall be much required."[20] Man worships God through service to men. This idea is embodied in a very familiar saying: "Learn the Truth and love men." This is one of the most familiar definitions or descriptions of a *Chun Tze* or the "princely man."[21]

4. *Life of Activity and Service.* Both put emphasis on a life of activity. One of the most frequently heard quotations in the Chinese language is that "learning is for use." Knowledge is not just for an intellectual pastime or for spiritual enjoyment. Although not in exactly the same language, Confucianism also teaches that we are to be in the world though not of the world, and should seek to improve the world. *Tao*, or Truth, must not remain in the abstract, but must realize and fulfill itself in *Teh*, virtue. The "talents" we receive from our Master must not merely be hid in the earth, but must be put in "trade"—to do good and benefit others. It was said of an ancient worthy (*E Yin*) that he felt overwhelmed by his responsi-

[19] Mencius, Bk. I. Pt. II. iii. 7.
[20] Luke 12:48.
[21] Analects xvii. 4.

192

bility of leadership because it was Heaven's purpose that the first enlightened must enlighten others, and the first awakened must awaken others, and that if any common man and woman had not come under the benevolent influence of *Yao* and *Shun*, the one who had been endowed with the quality of leadership must feel as if he had himself pushed them into a ditch.[22]

Confucianism, however, has much to learn from Christianity. It is good, but in itself it is not good enough and not complete enough to satisfy the full needs of man and mankind. The Christian Gospel is not only superior to Confucianism because it is the power of God unto salvation to all them that believe; but, even in its doctrinal aspect, it has many points which are superior to Confucianist teachings. The following may serve as illustrations.

1. *Conception of God*. Confucianism teaches that the Deity is the embodiment of goodness and justice, to be feared and respected by men as the ruler and judge of the universe; while Christianity teaches that God, in addition to being just and righteous, is also our loving Father, with whom men can enter into warm, intimate fellowship. In these troublesome days our thoughts will perhaps be less perplexed if we bear in mind that Christianity is

[22] Mencius, Bk. V. Pt. I. vii.

193

not love in substitution for, but love in addition to, justice and righteousness.

2. *Conception of Man.* Confucianism teaches that man is man, and the highest objective for him is to be a "princely man," an ideal or model gentleman; while Christianity teaches that man is the son of God, and should strive to be as perfect as his Father in heaven is perfect.

3. *Conception of an Ideal Society.* Confucius looked forward to a Kingdom of Justice and Righteousness; while Christianity looks forward to the Kingdom of God wherein, in addition to justice and righteousness, the love of God prevails.

4. *Message of Salvation.* Confucianism exhorts man to develop his moral character through self-cultivation and discipline; while Christianity preaches the gospel of salvation by the redeeming grace and power of Jesus Christ.

5. *Heritage to the World.* Confucianism gives to the world an excellent moral code, which can well serve as guiding principles for the construction of an orderly society; while Christianity gives to mankind a perfect life—the life of Jesus Christ our Lord, who is thoroughly adjusted in fellowship with God and devotion to the service of man, and who is the Truth and the way to an abundant life, even life eternal.

194

IV. The Centrality and Finality of Jesus Christ

What shall we say as a final thought on Christianity and the religions of China? Whether it is with reference to Confucianism or Buddhism or Taoism, this we may well say with Tennyson:

> Our little systems have their day;
> They have their day and cease to be;
> They are but broken lights of thee,
> And thou, O Lord, art more than they.

God indeed has not left himself without witness anywhere; but, at the same time, there is no other name than the name of our Lord Jesus Christ by whom man and mankind may be fully saved. China, like any other nation, has its "father Jacob and his well," and the Chinese, like the other peoples of the world, when brought face to face with Jesus Christ, may also ask the question, "Art thou greater than our father Jacob?" To them also the disciples of Jesus Christ may well answer for their Lord, "Whosoever drinketh of this water shall thirst again: but whosoever drinketh of the water that I shall give him shall never thirst; but the water . . . . shall be in him a well of water springing up into everlasting life."

Full salvation can come to the household of

195

China, as to the rest of mankind, only in proportion that the Chinese can be taught to say, as they look up to our Lord Jesus Christ, "Thou art the Christ, the Son of the living God."

As I write this final paragraph of this volume, my thoughts turn to the familiar story of the three Wise Men of the East who, on that first Christmas Eve, came to worship the newborn Saviour of mankind, and opened their treasures and presented unto him gifts—gold, and frankincense, and myrrh. How much I wish to imagine their names to be Confucius, Buddha, and Lao-tze! Can it ever be? According to our faith shall it be done unto us!

DATE DUE